My Therapist Is Making Me Nuts!

A Guide to Avoid Life's Obstacles

Mark Hillman, Ph.D.

Brookestone Publishing
Clifton Park, New York
2003

Library of Congress Control Number 2002094080

ISBN 0-9723774-0-9

Printed in the United States of America

Illustrated by
Jeanne A. Benas

To Linda

"A Woman of Valor"

Contents

Acknowledgements

My sincere appreciation to the corps of colleagues, staff and friends who provided guidance and support throughout this adventure. To Dr. Robert Penna, AKA "Bobby P" for his challenging me to write this book in "real" language and not get stuck in my own academic psychobabble. To Dr. William Danko for his support, encouragement, guidance and friendship. To Ms. JoAnn LeSage, AKA "Joey" for her editing skills and commitment to grammar and punctuation. To the corps of professionals at Whitston Publishing Co., especially Jill Wolcott for book layout and design. To Karen Rush, my administrative assistant for her countless hours of typing and retyping. To Jeanne Benas for her illustrations and book cover design; and lastly to Frank Busalacchi, AKA "Buca" for holding me accountable to write it.

Some opening thoughts . . .

ஃ ஃ ஃ

"You're gonna find this funny," he said, "but my shrink is making me **NUTS**."

"Oh?" I said, "how so?"

"Every week, it's the same thing: I talk and he listens. He takes a few notes, nods a lot, and when I'm done, he talks about stuff that has nothing to do with my problem. Repressed feelings, anger management, and communications. What does any of that have to do with me? Then there are the books he suggests. Men from this planet, women from that planet. I'm okay; you're not, on and on. The books don't tell me anything either. I swear, sometimes I think you therapists don't live in the real world. Just once I'd like my shrink to relate to my situation; just once I'd like to read one of those books and actually recognize the people they're talking about. Just once."

When the conversation and our lunch were over and my friend had left, I got to thinking about what he'd said. Were therapists and all the books we write and recommend that out of touch with the real problems our patients face? Are we so isolated in our models and paradigms that we offer solutions and analyses that have little to do with the every-day lives of the people who come to us looking for help?

I wondered.

I also took another hard look at the rows and rows of books that line the shelves of my office and home. I took some of them down and began to reread them. My friend, I thought, had a valid point.

And so, I started to rethink the models I use in my practice. I decided to rethink the way I analyzed my patients' various, but similar situations. And, I became determined to write this book.

"**Oh great, Mark**," I can hear you saying. "Just what we need, another book."

Well, I like to think that maybe you do need this book, or at least that maybe it'll help. You see, this book is different, and I'll tell you why.

No, this book isn't going to make you more beautiful or handsome. It isn't going to make you an instant business success (although it will help you recognize some things that might be standing in the way of that success). And it isn't going to solve every single problem you have with your spouse or significant other, your kids, your boss, your neighbor or your blowhard brother-in-law. If you want a book that does all that, one that will solve every single problem, go back to the shelves and look for something under philosophy, religion or Martha Stewart.

What this book will do, however, is help you recognize some of the stumbling blocks we all trip over time and again throughout our lives. Remember the opening credit sequence of the old *Dick Van Dyke Show*? Remember how he'd come in every week, be greeted by Mary Tyler Moore and then trip over the ottoman and fall down on his way to greet Morey Amsterdam and

Rose Marie? Didn't you just want to scream at the TV screen and warn him to watch out for that damned ottoman? Well, this book is a lot like that. Every year, every month, every week, and sometimes every day, we trip over the same psychic and emotional ottomans again and again. We get frustrated in our personal and professional relationships, we have our feelings hurt, we feel put upon and manipulated. We may change jobs; we may change relationship partners or even spouses. And yet, the next thing we know, we have that same argument all over again. We feel frustrated, under-appreciated and undervalued again; we get mad at ourselves and mad at others, and we look for reasons why. But the problem is that we often look in the wrong places.

Worse still, often the therapists and the books we turn to for help are among those wrong places because they are not focused on the real world in which we live. What's wrong with them? I think the problem is that a lot of well-meaning therapists and authors start with a model and then try to apply that model to a wide range of problems and situations. But just as there really isn't any one-size-fits-all garment that really fits everyone equally well, there is no one model that fits all situations. Rather, each situation and type of relationship is different, or at least has different dynamics at play. I wrote a moment ago about the ottoman Dick Van Dyke used to trip over and I said it is a lot like what many of us do repeatedly. But the more accurate truth is that we have a series of psychic and emotional obstacles we stumble over as we go through the days and weeks of our lives. It would be as though poor Dick tripped over the ottoman in the living room, a misplaced stool in the kitchen, Richie's fire truck in the hall and Laura's shoes in the bedroom. Remembering that the ottoman was in the living room would not be enough to spare him the daily tumbles over all those other things.

I wrote this book to help you recognize the things you might be stumbling over not just in one place or in one facet of your life, but in several. I wrote this book to help you look for answers in the right places for a change. What are the right places? Most of them are right there, inside you, inside me, inside all of us. Also, some of them are in the outside world, in the society and rules with which we grew up and live. Rarely, however, is the answer found in another person, so forget looking there. **There is no perfect mate, perfect spouse or perfect boss. There is no perfect job, no perfect career and no perfect situation**. But none of that means that you have to be miserable; there are ways to be happy in spite of the fact that nothing in this life is perfect and few things are always the way we want them to be.

So how do you find them? In this book, I am going to suggest essentially one strategy; I call it **facilitating your environment**. What does that mean? It means, in essence, getting rid of the ottomans (and the fire trucks, the misplaced stools and boots) that are in your way, the hidden (and not-so-hidden) obstacles that lie, like landmines, just waiting for you to come along and trip over them, step on them or otherwise set them off.

As you read this book, I am going to introduce you to a lot of new concepts. Some of which you will recognize easily and realize that you just never had a name for them before. You will, I hope, recognize a lot of the situations presented and maybe even recognize yourself in them. Others you may have to think about for a while before you see how they impact you in your everyday personal and professional lives. Sometimes, it may seem that I am wandering a bit far afield; but I promise you that when I do it is to make a point and I will always bring you back to the main discussion. Finally, this book will ask you a lot of questions, questions designed to make you think, make you analyze and, hopefully, help you be honest with yourself.

There is a great line in an old song: "**The strongest lies are always those, the ones we tell ourselves**. . . ." So that is where we are going to begin. We are going to examine the lies we tell ourselves, notions such as **operating fantasies, operating assumptions and operating presumptions**. We are going to examine the **parallel value tracks** each of us has in his or her life, how we use them to make decisions and how others often use them against us. We are going to take a look at **effective control**, at **growing up** versus **maturing**; we are going to discuss **well-defined outcomes**. We will discuss **denial**, the **degrees of control** we have over our lives, the concepts of **motivation, currencies of approval and currencies of gratification**, the differences between **recognition** and **reward**, between **reaction** and **response, blame vs. responsibility** and the notion of **My Nice vs. Your Nice**, among other ideas. And, we are going to do it with **humor**.

Along the way, you will meet such characters as the Unfortunate Jones, his wife and her fish sticks. You will meet Ol' Stuffenbottom, the quintessential boss. You'll meet Cobblepot and Bixby. We'll make stops in Oz and the Twilight Zone, and have a point or two made by Mr. Spock. I want this book to be entertaining, as well as engaging.

A good deal of this book takes the form of a dialogue. I am trying to communicate with you in this book, so I couch the entire thing as a conversation between us.

I think it is a format with which you will be comfortable; it is relaxed, informal and, I hope, constructive.

Eventually, if you remember the show, even Dick Van Dyke learned to avoid the ottoman and stopped tripping over it during those opening credits. It is my hope that, after reading this book, you will find that you, too, have finally found a way around some of the obstacles that repeatedly have blocked your path to personal and professional fulfillment. The journey toward that goal begins when you turn this page.

CHAPTER 1

You're Not in Kansas Anymore

❧ ❧ ❧

I am what they call a cognitive-behavioral therapist. What does that mean in plain English? Simply this:
I believe that human beings never do anything sponta-
neously. Thought always precedes action. So, to make
active changes, you have to change your thoughts first.
Sound simple? Well, in some ways, it is!

Do you remember the story of *The Wizard of Oz*?
Lou Tice, author of *Investment in Excellence*, uses the plot
of that movie as a metaphor to make a point I would like
to share with you. In the story, we meet Dorothy, Toto,
the Scarecrow, the Tin Man and the Cowardly Lion. They
go to visit the Wizard who lives in the Land of Oz. They
have all sorts of adventures, but essentially the goal of
their journey is to make themselves "**more worthy**." The
others perceive the Wizard as all-powerful. He has the
ability to grant them what they need, what they have
longed for. So, it's a great disappointment and surprise
when Toto pulls back the curtain, and all they see is an
ordinary little man spinning dials and pulling levers. It
turns out that their expectations aren't met. There's no

magical wizard, after all. In fact, at best, the wizard is neutral. He isn't bad. He isn't good. He's false. Period. End of story.

Dorothy, the Tin Man and the others may have believed in his power, but that didn't make his power real. Sure, it made life easier for a while to think someone or something could make every problem disappear, that it was possible to live happily ever after, but it didn't help much in real terms. When push came to shove, the little man and his pulling levers provided nothing. The Lion still needed courage, and the Scarecrow needed brains. Dorothy still longed for home, and the Tin Man couldn't get the heart he wanted. Believing and **thinking** that the Wizard had power was what prompted this group's pilgrimage. In other words, **a thought** (about the power of the Wizard) led to the **action** (going to find the Wizard). But that misguided thought also led to a dead end.

As children, we were misled. Like Dorothy and the Munchkins, we saw our futures through rose-colored glasses. From romance novels to movies, to dreams about what we wanted to be when we grew up, we got the message that through some unspecified combination of hard work and good luck, we could have it all. So, when asked what we wanted our lives to be like, we answered in the context of what we believed our lives could be. Did we answer that we wanted to live in a cramped apartment, dragging our sorry selves through the daily grind of a dead-end job? No! Did we answer that we wanted to experience the grief of failed romances, of sickness and death, of betrayal, economic downsizing or the countless smaller disappointments we face in daily life? Of course not! We told our questioners the truth. We wanted to be firemen or nurses and to be married and happy and rich when we grew up.

We wanted a house with a white picket fence, and we said so. We wanted kids. We wanted a successful career, a loving relationship, a fun sex life, a chicken in every pot, and a two-car garage. These ideals were day-dreams and we never questioned any of them until the **disillusionment** and **disenchantment** of unmet expecta-tions started, slowly but surely, to accumulate. In other words, we started to grow up. It can be difficult to rec-oncile, but in many ways, **growing up means growing disappointed**.

Take for instance, a normal 13-year-old. School, teachers, parents, the weather—**life!**—are deemed com-pletely unfair. Why? Usually the 13-year-old is experi-encing, in very real terms, that the stakes are getting high-er, and that his or her parents don't have the ability to fix everything, to make everything alright. The 13-year-old voices his or her frustration with this reality by proclaim-ing **everything and everyone unfair**.

From the first broken toy that can't be fixed to the first home run we don't hit, from the first unrequited love to the first job we don't get, we all learn slowly that life isn't fair. Yet, this rarely puts an end to our *operating fan-tasies*. What is an operating fantasy? In short, it's an unre-alistic expectation, an idea or ideal that we don't question. It's the "wizard" we seek, believing without really think-ing it through. Ironically, when we are disappointed we don't abandon operating fantasies. On the contrary, we simply trade in one operating fantasy for another. We trade in the fantasy of a perfect teenage life for fantasies about the upcoming, independent, fun years we'll have in our twenties. And when that turns out to be misguided, we believe that family life with a house and kids will solve our problems, that true happiness will be found there. In other words, like Dorothy and her friends, we trade one false wizard in for another. We believe that we'll get a driver's license, we'll graduate, we'll buy beer and that, somehow, it all will work out.

Are we right? You tell me.

When the Wizard says to the Scarecrow, "By the power vested in me, I grant you this diploma—now go act smart," when he says to the Lion, "By the power vested in me I grant you this medal of courage—now go act brave!" does it work? Does it happen? Maybe in the movies, but in real life, when we are proclaimed adults— "now go act mature!"—we find ourselves stunned, with jaws dropped, eyes open wide, muttering "**Huh**?"

We've never been adults before. We don't really know what to do. All our previous life experience has been that of a child and adolescent. We're still attached to the operating fantasies we formed while growing up. We haven't replaced them with anything new. So, somehow, some way, somewhere, in spite of a lot of experience to the contrary, we still expect life to be fair.

The truth is that just as the Wizard's commands to "Go act brave" and "Go act smart" were arbitrary and ridiculous, the priest's or rabbi's command to "Go act married" after a wedding ceremony is arbitrary and ridiculous, too. If you've never been married before, how do you know how to be married? If you've failed at marriage once, how do you prevent it from happening again?

You can't know automatically how to be an adult or to be married unless you know what to expect. Expecting perfection, expecting your life to be like a movie, expecting your childhood dreams to come true, is to expect—well, disaster.

The key is to recognize these operating fantasies and to replace them with realistic expectations instead. How do you go about doing such a thing? I wish the answer were a short one. But, come along. In the next chapter, we'll discuss different types of expectations and what they can mean for you.

❦ ❦ ❦

Exercise:

(Please write down your answers to the following questions. Yes, it's okay to write in the book.)

Think back to your childhood. What is the first thing you wanted to be when you grew up?

Teacher

Who were the powerful wizards in your life? Both positive and negative?

Mom

Recall your first major disappointment. When did you start to realize that your parents or caregivers couldn't fix everything?

College

CHAPTER 2

When You Wish Upon a Star

ॐ ॐ ॐ

We have briefly discussed how having unmet expectations leads to various manifestations of frustration, and we will go into this at greater length later. But, for now, **a question we must ask is whether having expectations is, in and of itself, a bad thing.** By having expectations do we merely set ourselves up for disappointment again and again? Would it not be better to simply go through life expecting nothing, viewing each day as a crapshoot, a roll of the dice during which anything might happen? Well, the answer is yes and no.

The key is to understand that there are **different types of expectations.** In simple terms, we can say there are **three** basic types of expectations: *operating fantasies, operating assumptions* and *operating presumptions.* As mentioned in Chapter One, an operating fantasy is an unrealistic expectation, an idea or ideal we don't question. An **operating assumption** is an expectation based on probability and an **operating presumption** is the gray area between what we expect will happen and what we hope will happen.

When we go to work in the morning, we assume that the office will be there. We assume that on payday, we will get a check for the amount we have earned. When we return home from work at night, we assume that our spouse or partner, our children, the dog and the goldfish will still be there. When we call our best friend to chat, or initiate sex with our lover or spouse, we assume that the reaction will be positive. When we visit the doctor, the lawn mower repairman and the dry cleaner, we assume that they know their business and will provide professional service. The list goes on and on . . . but what does it tell us?

In short, these examples illustrate that certain everyday, mundane expectations—our daily operating assumptions—allow us to function without having to constantly go back and reestablish the relationships, the rules, the basic parameters of our lives. They are what allow life to go on and, in this way, they work! Imagine a life without them. We'd be perpetually suspicious, fearful, and naive, waking each morning anxious about negotiating the world we left behind the night before. Without these assumptions, functioning in society, holding a job, or having a normal relationship would be virtually impossible. So, yes, operating assumptions make getting through each day possible.

An **operating assumption** is based on experience, on probability. We know, of course, going back to our earlier examples, that it is possible that we could arrive at work only to find that the office building had burned down the night before. It is possible that our check will be missing or that the amount will be grossly incorrect. It is possible that our partner will leave, the doctor is a quack, or that the dry cleaner will ruin our favorite suit. It is possible. But it is not probable. In the normal course of events, most of these misfortunes will not be ours.

In this way, an operating assumption differs greatly from an operating fantasy. Operating assumptions are grounded in reality. The operating assumption, for example, that going to college will better prepare us for a good job or career differs from the operating fantasy that, having completed a degree, we will land a $150,000 job within our first few interviews. The operating assumption that assumes if we develop an active social life eventually we will meet someone we find appealing is realistic; the operating fantasy that predicts a beautiful, rich, intelligent, sexy, vivacious person will suddenly appear, declare undying devotion and sweep us off our feet is not. The operating assumption that assumes investing in a mutual fund with a good track record will result in a positive return differs from the operating fantasy that believes if we pour $20 a week into tickets and buy Guaranteed Mystic Winning Number Books at the supermarket checkout counter we are going to win $25 million in the lottery.

We can laugh at these examples of operating fantasies. After all, we recognize that the skinny, undersized 13-year-old who—having never before been interested in, played or even watched a football game—suddenly catches football fever, starts wearing an NFL team jacket, announces that he is going to be a kicker on the high school team next year and grow up to be a professional kicker is acting out a fantasy. We smile an indulgent smile as his practice kick lands the ball on the roof yet again, knowing that in all probability the dream won't come true . . . if it even survives the school year. We understand and accept the fantasy because he is only 13. Yet, in our own ways, we all do exactly the same thing.

Don't most of us assume that "for richer, for poorer, 'til death us do part" means exactly that—that marriage is forever? Don't we assume that if we do a good job at work, we will be rewarded and not find our careers cut short by capricious whim or fate? Don't most parents assume that their children will grow up to be healthy and content and strong?

The answer to those questions may be yes, but remember: The gambler assumes that the next game, the next horse, the next roll of the dice will bring Lady Luck back to his side.

The human facility to peer into the future and bet that what we want to happen actually will is called **hope**, something we all need just to get out of bed in the morning. Problems arise, however, when the line between what we hope will happen and what we absolutely expect will happen is blurred. When what we hope for impairs our ability to recognize warning signs that suggest a different outcome, when it prevents us from changing course or simply stopping, when our hopes are simply too high, **life can get dangerous**.

In fact, living that way means you may have crossed into altogether different territory entirely, into something called *denial*. What, exactly, is denial? **Most simply put, denial is the active refusal to accept what is**. It has become somewhat fashionable over the last several years to term all sorts of people as being "in denial." And sometimes they are. The substance abuser who refuses to accept that he or she has a problem is in denial. The abused wife who repeatedly accepts her husband's assertions that the abuse is somehow her fault is in denial. There are numerous examples we could cite. But, for the purposes of our discussion, let's get a few things straight about what denial is *not*.

Denial is not the same as forgiveness. Someone

may actively choose to forgive, overlook or simply accept the abusive or negative behavior of another person. This does not mean that the person in question fails to see that the other person's behavior is abusive or negative. It does not mean that he or she is in denial. Rather, he or she is aware of it and recognizes it for what it is. But, he or she, using an internal calculus of value, benefits, and losses, actively chooses to accept that behavior.

Denial is also not the same as thinking that we can change a person or situation. Countless examples of couples who have entered relationships, each thinking that they could "**change**" the other, can be cited. Denial is not occurring here because recognition that there is some pattern of behavior in the other person that needs changing is present. It may be a fool's errand and a waste of time (or a life) to try, but it is not denial.

Rather, denial is the refusal to process evidence we have at hand that is contrary to our image of a person or situation. The person who enters a relationship and continually sublimates or ignores evidence that his or her significant other is a habitual liar is, probably, in denial. Similarly, the person who ignores evidence that his or her significant other's past is not what he or she said it was, and goes on to ignore strong hints that negative traces of the person's true past behavior patterns are still in evidence, can also be said to be in denial.

Is denial the same as believing in yourself when no one else does? Does the fact that no one else thinks you have a chance in hell of successfully becoming a singer mean you are in denial if you pursue your dream? If you are 20 and working full time at honing the skills and performance of your band, then no, you are probably not in denial. However, if you are 45, have never held a job and never passed an audition, if the only crowds you've ever played are in the audience of your ever-fertile imagination, then denial could be an apt description of your assessment of your never-quite-budding musical career. But this brings us to another point, and full circle in our larger discussion of the difference between operating fantasies and operating assumptions.

Denial of what is is quite often coupled with an equally active preference for what might be or what could be. This is the **root** of the **operating fantasy**: a refusal to accept, to even mentally or emotionally process the facts of the way things are in deference to a vision of the way things could be, ought to be, or the way we believe them to be.

But does recognizing this essential difference between an operating fantasy and an operating assumption mean that people should have no fantasies, that we should live our lives never entertaining wistful thoughts of what might have been, of what might one day happen? Certainly not.

On the contrary, research suggests that fantasies or daydreams are a natural and beneficial part of our overall emotional and psychological make up. Sexual fantasies, for example, about people or situations can be a helpful addition to a healthy sexual relationship between two people. Fantasizing about putting the boss you find so frustrating in his place, about punching an officious cop in the nose, or about running away to the South Seas can be a healthy way to relieve stress. But actually acting on those daydreams, acting them out or even attempting to arrange for them to happen can lead to disaster.

A 40-year-old man may engage in the **Jimmy Buffet Syndrome** and harbor daydreams of leaving his job, his wife and the kids in favor of an idle life spent drinking margaritas, chasing women, and living on a leaky old shrimp boat, but he'd be an idiot (not to mention irresponsible) if he actually quit his job, left his wife and kids, and headed down to the Keys in search of that lost shaker of salt. A middle-aged college professor may similarly fantasize about a threesome with two of his nubile, young students, but getting caught attempting to arrange such a liaison would probably not sit well with either the school administration or the good professor's wife. And as for punching the cop in the nose. . . .

Luckily, most people recognize the difference between having or even enjoying this sort of fantasy and acting upon it; those who don't recognize the difference, on the other hand, tend to find themselves in trouble. Either way, most people recognize the dangers to their lives and livelihood in acting upon these impulses and simply, wisely, choose not to act. It is interesting, then, that many of these same people fail to recognize the equal danger inherent in acting upon or counting on the fulfillment of long-held, almost subconscious operating fantasies. Specifically, while most people know the difference between fantasizing about hitting the boss and actually hitting him, they don't recognize the difference between hoping their careers or marriages will be successful, and actually making the changes and compromises necessary to make sure that they are successful.

The key is to recognize the difference between what we wish would happen and what is likely to happen, between outcomes over which we have at least some degree of control and those entirely, irrevocably, and forever out of our hands.

This raises two additional points that we'll discuss next: the difference between what we can and cannot control.

❦ ❦ ❦

Exercise:

(That's right, we write in the book again.)

When we were young, most of us had a dream about what we were going to grow up to be; those were perhaps our first operating fantasies. What did you think you were going to be when you grew up? happy, Kids pretty $

Where did you think you might live? Next Door to Mom

Did you imagine yourself married or single? M

What was that fantasy based upon? (Was it based upon an image you got from TV, the movies, sports heroes, gender stereotyping or romance novels?) TV movies

How close to those dreams did reality turn out to be? picture-perfect really-not (no love)

How great is the difference between the dream and the reality?

Love is difference

*Now think about how you will probably spend your next holi-
day. Is that expectation based upon past tradition, upon how
you usually spend your holidays?*

*Last xmas — very marginal
next xmas — hopefully better*

*Is the expectation based upon arrangements you have already
made?*

No

*If so, do you begin to see how the operating assumption about
your next holiday differs from your childhood operating fantasy about what you'd be when you grew up? Do you see how
the holiday assumption is based upon something concrete—in
this case perhaps tradition—while the fantasy was based upon
desire?*

*Make a list of some other things you have wished for or expect-
ed during your life. They can be great or small wishes or expectations.*

1. happy marriage   T/F   VE/WT
2. happy family   T/F   VE/WT
3. health — met family   T/F   VE/WT
4. successful business   T/F   VE/WT
5. a few friends   T/F   VE/WT

Now, next to each item, make a note of whether it came true or did not. Which of the things you listed were true, valid expectations based upon probability, and which were merely wishful thinking based upon little more than desire? Can you see a difference?

CHAPTER 3

Next Stop: The Twilight Zone

ॠ ॠ ॠ

As Rod Serling used to remind us each week, there are gray places in life, areas "not of sight and sound, **but of mind**" that often crop up, befuddling our everyday expectations. For many of us, that gray area lies between what we have been referring to as operating fantasy and operating assumption, the times and places in our personal and professional lives that appear to give us every reason to believe that an expected outcome will be positive. Most often, these are things we count on without ever admitting to ourselves that we are, in fact, counting on them coming to pass.

At the same time, there is another, parallel, gray area between our vision of what we want and the reality of what we want. To deal with these two connected issues, I am going to break this chapter into two sections for a moment. In the first we'll discuss what I call the *operating presumption*. Following that, I'll turn our attentions to the gulf between what we think we want and how we react when we get it. For now, let's examine the operating presumption.

While there are innumerable examples of this **"gray area,"** perhaps none is more familiar to most people than the events surrounding a date.

How many of us have had what we thought was a wonderful first date, only to end up being surprised and hurt when the other person either seems to cut the date short or never calls back? How many times after a great, even romantic evening, have we been surprised and wounded, even angered, to find that the other person does not extend any sort of invitation to "continue the evening" after dinner or a show? What is going on in situations like these?

Are the wounded parties in these illustrations victims of unrealistic operating fantasies? Unless the situation involved a celebrity date with a movie star won in a contest, probably not. Rather, the people who fit into this example have simply fallen prey to a third category of expectation, the **operating presumption**, that gray, foggy area between fantasy and assumption. An operating presumption is based on a risky mixture of fact and fancy, a combination of a realistic and well-grounded assessment of what will happen and a wish for what might happen. The assumption in the dating scenario was that if the man or woman went out, dressed and acted his or her best and observed certain social norms, the evening would go pleasantly. Interestingly, that is what usually happens. Then why are they so unhappy? I would suggest that the problem is the operating presumption each person carried into the date.

The presumption was that **rewards** would follow once the immediate goal was realized. Disappointment did not arise because the evening was not a success. The evening was a success. Rather, disappointment arose from the fact that the further expectations, the presumptions of what would follow, were not met. In this case, either he was not invited inside when he brought his date home or she did not receive a call inviting her to a follow-up date.

· Nor should anyone think that such misfired expectations occur only in our personal lives. Our professional lives, too, offer countless opportunities for us to stick our necks out in the expectation (hope?) that a positive result will follow.

Perhaps no example is as common as the job interview. Let's use a man named Bixby as our example. Bixby needs a job. He had a great career, until he and his position were downsized out of the firm. But with solid credentials and a well-documented mastery of his field, Bixby sets out to secure another position. He does everything right. He has a new resume written and professionally printed. He works his network of contacts, peruses the *New York Times* job listings every week and goes on-line to seek out even more opportunities. Finally, he gets invited for the big interview. He does an incredible amount of research into the prospective employer's operation. He goes into the interview fresh, confident and armed with facts, figures and an action plan to demonstrate his command of what needs to be done in the position for which he is interviewing. He blows 'em away in the interview. They shake his hand; they tell him how impressive he is. They give the job to someone else. Bixby is crushed.

On the other hand, let's consider Cobblepot. Cobblepot runs a small- to mid-sized ad agency. A Major Concern in his area announces its intention to award a multi-million dollar contract. Cobblepot decides to go after that contract. He hires the best outside talent he can find to help him put together his firm's presentation.

Going beyond mere art, design, and copy, he brings in as consultants experts in the field the Major Concern is involved with to ensure that he and his team have the appropriate jargon down, know the ins and outs of the industry, and know precisely what the Major Concern needs in its new campaign. Altogether, Cobblepot spends over $15,000 on his presentation.

When the day of the big presentation finally arrives, Cobblepot and his team are ready. They have charts. They have slides. They have a video to show. They have demographics. They have it all. At the presentation, the screening committee is in awe. The say "Oooo" and "Ahhh" at the charts, the slides, and the video presentation. They nod knowingly and approvingly at the demographics. The presentation is everything Cobblepot could have hoped it would be. The only problem is that the multi-million dollar contract is awarded to a firm across the river, a firm that happens to be owned by the nephew of the Major Concern's chairman of the board.

In all these cases, the people involved were disappointed. Their egos were bruised and, perhaps, their sense of self damaged. Added to this is Bixby's worsening financial situation and the $15,000 Cobblepot blew on the presentation.

Again we ask, what is going on here? On an emotional, human scale, we can certainly understand their disappointment. But, their psychological reactions to these events are more important. The immediately reactive emotions will, no doubt, pass. **But, the psychological reactions can have a lasting impact**. The disappointed woman may find herself rejecting dates in a certainty that she will only be hurt again. The disappointed man may begin to develop a hostile attitude toward women.

Bixby may drop out of the job market altogether and Cobblepot may never again put forth the effort needed to land that really big account. In other words, each may draw the wrong lesson from the disappointment he or she experienced.

Let's use another example. Imagine a man named Jones is given a very important, very sensitive assignment at work. His **operating assumption** is that if he is diligent and does what he is supposed to do, the project will turn out well and the boss will be pleased. In this, he is correct and things do, indeed, turn out this way upon his completion of the assignment. The boss is happy and Jones, for the moment, is happy that the boss is happy. But thereafter Jones is disappointed, indeed shocked and appalled, to find that he does not get a bonus, does not get a bigger office, and does not get the promotion he expected would follow his completion of the important and sensitive assignment. He is wounded, embarrassed, hurt, and resentful. Why? Because he went beyond the rational assumption of what would follow his doing a good job. The assumption was that the boss would be pleased. So far, so good. He had control over this part of the equation.

But he had **no control** over what he hoped would follow . . . that part where the boss' pleasure would translate into a **further reward**. This, therefore, was the **presumption . . . that a reward would follow**. This presumption unmet, Jones was unfulfilled, hurt, and unhappy.

To further understand this, we must recognize that we all have expectations we carry with us every day, be they operating fantasies, operating assumptions or operating presumptions. We have expectations about certain types of situations, about fidelity, finances, sex, professionalism, about people being on time. We have these ideals about a world filled with people and situations, as they ought to be. We have a similarly unrealistic image of our own perfection and the perfect lives for which we strive. For that reason, we face each day pre-armed with hundreds and hundreds of expectations whether we are consciously aware of them or not. The expectation could be as mundane as finding mail in the mailbox, or as specific and poignant as Charlie Brown's futile expectation every Valentine's Day that the mailbox will (finally) hold a card from the Little Red-Headed Girl. The expectation could be as commonplace as expecting hot water when we turn on the shower. Or the expectation could be as emotionally laden as hoping to run into that one Great Flame (and perhaps even rekindle the spark) at our 20th high school reunion.

Either way, though, when our expectations about a situation are unmet, whatever those expectations may be, what usually happens is that we experience an **ego bruise**.

On the rare occasion when our expectations are negative and things turn out well, we are pleased. But more often we are hoping for things to turn out better than they actually do. Depending upon how much stock we placed in the expectations in the first place, we can be significantly "bruised" by the way things turn out.

When we say that you have experienced an **ego bruise**, it means that someone or some set of circumstances has taken your sense of who you are and what you expect from a situation and stepped on it, bruising you in the process. It's only after we experience this ego bruise that we experience a **primary negative emotion**. Hurt, rejection, disappointment, despair, helplessness are all manifestations of this primary emotion.

But the essential question to ask here is whether all ego bruises are equally valid.

"Now wait a minute, Mark," you might object. "Are you saying that I have no right to be insulted when I am treated badly or with disrespect?"

No, that is not what I am saying, precisely. But what I am saying is that we often set ourselves up for a bruise by the expectations, the presumptions we have of a situation.

Let's look at it this way: if someone insults you in Russian, Turkish or Klingonese, do you experience a wound? Probably not, because the chances are you do not understand Russian, Turkish or Klingonese. In other words, your brain, your ego, your sense of self does not process the insult, so it has no impact on you. **It simply does not compute**.

Yet, just as we can be deliberately insulted but not feel or process the insult, we can also experience an insult or ego bruise where none was **intended**. Why? Because of our presumptions about what the situation will yield. When those presumptions go unmet, we very often experience an ego bruise. But we must ask whether the person "responsible" for that bruise had any notion of what our presumptions were, or whether they were at all valid. Did we have a right to expect a further benefit, something beyond our presumably valid operating assumption, from this situation?

For a bit more clarity, let's return to the unfortunate and so recently bruised Jones. As we have seen, Jones is disappointed, indeed shocked and appalled, to learn that he did not get a bonus, did not get a bigger office, and did not get the promotion he expected would follow his successful and outstanding completion of the very important and very sensitive assignment. As we noted, he is wounded, embarrassed, hurt, and resentful. Why? As Jones views it, he has experienced an ego bruise.

Beyond his operating assumption concerning the immediate outcome of his performance, it turns out that Jones, whether in the privacy of his own thoughts or perhaps in conversation with his friends, co-workers, and Mrs. Jones, **presumed** that some positive outcome would be a further or extended result of his actions. Jones, in other words, went past the rational, realistic assumption about an outcome over which he had some degree of control—namely that the assignment would be a success if he did what he was supposed to do—to a presumption about an outcome over which he had **no control**, namely the action that would be taken by his boss . . . some sort of concrete reward. His presumption that the boss would show his pleasure in some concrete way beyond a hearty "Good job," and a pat on the back was unmet when the pat on the back was all the boss gave him. In the case of the daters we mentioned earlier, he presumed that a kiss on the cheek at her front door would not be the way the evening ended. She presumed that he'd call again. In both these cases and the case of the woebegone Jones, it was the operating presumption, not the operating assumption that was left unmet. The unmet presumption led to the ego bruise, but it was the presumption itself that set each party up to be bruised in the first place.

In these examples, we should also note, several identifiable confusions can be identified. The first is the **confusion between assumption and presumption**. The second is confusion over the essential difference between **recognition and reward**. Add to these the issue of control over one's environment, and you have a recipe for unnecessary disappointment!

We've been discussing the confusion between a

valid operating assumption and a shakier operating presumption. But what about the difference between recognition and reward?

Let's once again visit the woeful Mr. Jones. We have established that he is hurt when he learns he did not receive the **further benefits he presumed** would follow his completion of the assignment. We also established, however, that his boss did recognize the fact that Jones had achieved the immediate goal of successfully completing the task at hand. Thus, Jones did receive recognition; what he felt he did not receive, however, was a reward. This differentiation between recognition and reward is crucial to the concept we are discussing, for it lies at the heart of how operating presumptions often fail us.

Here's another example: A husband leaves work early on Friday afternoon to stop by the fish market to buy some shrimp. Getting home after stopping by the wine shop for an exquisite Pinot Grigio, he lights some candles and prepares a wonderful dinner to surprise his wife. She gets home a bit late after having been caught in traffic, sees what he's doing, and says "Oh, that's so nice of you," and goes inside to change. They have dinner, during which she never particularly remarks about the meal he has prepared beyond simply telling him it is good, and the rest of the evening passes. Burned out from her day at work, a bit after eight she announces she is retiring early, kisses him on the cheek and goes to bed. Now, what is the husband feeling?

He looks at the dirty dishes still sitting in the sink, glances at the glass of wine she hardly touched, looks down the hall at the closed bedroom door, and decides that his efforts were wasted. He blows out the candles, pours a double vodka on the rocks, leaves the dishes in the sink (quietly thinking "Let her clean them up in the morning") and slumps into his armchair to watch reruns of "Baywatch."

The next morning, slightly hung over, he is grumpy and appears, at least to his wife, a total mystery. **"What the heck did I do wrong this time**?" she wonders, defensively. What has gone on here?

Quite simply, the husband overlooked his wife's recognition of his efforts. She not only commented that it was nice of him to make dinner, she told him the meal was good. But the husband ignored this, and focused instead on the fact that his **presumed reward**, a wild night of candlelight, wine, and passion, had gone unfulfilled. She, meanwhile, having missed his cues because she'd had a horrible day at work, got caught in traffic, and had a pounding headache, can't fathom why he would make such a nice gesture on Friday night, then growl at her on Saturday morning.

Recognition has an intrinsic value, but it is a value we usually overlook in our focus upon the further payoff we are so busily anticipating. In other words, in examining our innate feelings of frustration in a situation—often the result of our presumptions not being realized—we must ask whether we are overlooking the recognition we actually received in our frantic search for the **reward** we hoped to receive. In order to be honest with ourselves, therefore, we have to ask each time we experience frustration or an ego bruise whether we are ignoring recognition of our achievement in favor of focusing upon an unmet desire for a reward. This is the confusion between reward and recognition.

But we also mentioned that part of Jones' problem was the confusion between those things over which he had control and those over which he had little or no control. We need to examine this next.

In the example of Mr. Jones, his reward equation went something like this:

Jones Does Good Job + Boss' Impulse to Reward
=Promotion or Other Benefit

But, over what parts of that equation did Jones have even the slightest measure of control? Well, Jones could influence a measure of control over the quality of the work he did on the project. He could control the amount of overall effort he put into the project. He could control the amount of time he spent on background research and the amount of time he spent on the project's report and presentation. On these matters, Jones definitely had control. But what about the other part of the equation, the part having to do with the Boss' reaction to the fabulous job Jones did?

Here, unfortunately for Jones, we find that he had no control whatsoever. Perhaps the Boss saw Jones' performance as merely what was to be expected from a professional of Jones' caliber. Perhaps the Boss did not believe in bonuses or rewards. It could be that the Boss' budget and organizational structure did not allow for a cash bonus, a raise, or a promotion. Over none of these things did Jones have even the slightest bit of control. And yet, fully one-half of Jones' reward equation, his operating presumption, rested on the Boss' reaction.

Let's look once again at our frustrated daters. Each did what he or she could to make the evening a success. And it was a success. However, she had no control over whether the man she dated wanted anything more than a casual relationship. She had no control over whether there might be another woman in whom he might be more interested. She had no control over whether he was emotionally open to a more serious relationship, as might be indicated by a second date. Ultimately, she had no control over whether or not she would ignite an emotional spark in him. Therefore, her reward equation, the basis of her operating presumption, was crippled from the outset, because she had no control over anything other than her contribution to a pleasant evening.

Similarly, he had no control over whether she would even consider inviting him in to continue the evening. Perhaps she was just tired. Perhaps she felt that such an invitation would put her in a compromising position.

Either way, his reward equation:

**I Am Pleasant + Her Desire for . . . =
My Reward (being invited inside)**

This is faulty because he had no control over what she would do once he got her to her doorstep.

And so we must ask, how often are we disappointed in not receiving a reward over which we have no control? How often do we experience an ego bruise because we had our hearts set on receiving something, the attainment of which was beyond our powers to effect? Oh, to be sure, in these cases we get mad at the Boss, at Him or Her, because we see that person as responsible for the hurt or disappointment we have experienced. But is it really the other person who is responsible? Or have we, by virtue of our unfounded operating presumptions, set up the conditions for the disappointment, all but guarantying that it would occur?

Remember, this is significantly different from the hurt or disappointment we experience when an operating assumption goes unmet or unfulfilled. Recall that an operating assumption is based on concrete experience and probability. It is something we are justified in expecting to happen. The expectation of a weekly paycheck is an example. If, for some reason, it is missing on payday, we may experience a range of negative emotions, and in this we'd be justified. But with an operating presumption we go beyond experience and probability into the realm of wishful thinking. It is because of this that we must ask whether our negative feeling, our anger, resentment, and our ego bruise are valid. Because if they are not, then we must also ask whether it makes sense to continue experiencing these ego bruises and the pain associated with them.

"Now wait a minute, Mark," I can hear you saying. "I might not feel insulted if someone calls me a name in a language I don't understand, but that's a bit different than not getting the promotion I was hoping for. That still hurts no matter what."

Yeah, I know . . . it does. But, the key here is what the "hope" was based on. For one thing, was it truly a **hope** (which is essentially a "wish")? Or was it an **"expectation?"** In the examples we cited, Jones and the two daters, their operating presumptions went beyond a hope or a wish. They had, indeed, blossomed into expectations. That is the essence of an operating presumption, the expectation. Only you can look at your life, its disappointments, and unmet desires and truly determine the extent to which they were the result of dashed hopes, unmet operating presumptions or unfulfilled but valid expectations. But the exercise of examining them may help you separate those cases in which you had every right to be hurt or disappointed from those when mere hope or presumption led you to expect a reward or other goodie you didn't get.

But before you examine that question, I am going to pose another sort of operating presumption for you to think about. I am going to suggest that sometimes what we presume is not that something will happen, but rather that nothing will happen.

Let's consider an illustration to make this a bit more clear. What happens, for example, when a relationship begins? When we first meet someone, there is a lot of formal behavior, and this is an important point to recognize. What is **formal behavior**? It is a ritualized pattern of actions, largely cultural in origin, accepted as appropriate and expected in certain social situations. You, therefore, are on your **best behavior**, and so is the person you are about to spend some time with. To a great extent, you're each presenting the best version—and only the best version—of who you are. Why?

Partially, it is because of the ritualized nature of how we are taught to behave with people we don't know all that well. Our mothers' admonition to "Sit up straight" when we were kids and perhaps having dinner with a distant relative or Dad's boss was an early example of this. At home with just Mom and Dad, we might have slouched at the dinner table and no one said anything because of the loose, comfortable and familiar situation. But with Great Aunt Maud or Mr. Stuffenbottom there to share the family pot roast, suddenly our mother's "Sit up" reminded us that this wasn't a loose and familiar situation and a more ritualized, formal behavior was expected. So we tried to remember to say "please" and "thank you," not wipe our mouths with our sleeve and not belch. So, too, on a first date, we remember not to slouch, not to belch and say, "Please pass the salt," rather than "Toss me the salt, would ya?"

We also do this, particularly in the earliest stages of

a relationship (or on a job interview) because, often, we believe that our "real" self might not be as impressive as our "formal" self. So we primp and perform. We act our best, sending chocolates or notes, opening doors, and making eye contact. The other person is similarly engaging and engaged. And after a few dates like this, we feel like we've finally found what we've been looking for all along: one of those charming and considerate, sexy and attentive partners like the ones in the movies and on TV.

The same scenario goes on in our professional lives as well during the first interview, the first client meeting, even when we use our professional voice to answer our business telephone. These are examples of **formal or best behavior**.

The down side of all this, of course, is that eventually, trait by trait, bits of informal, less perfect behavior trickle into these formal relationships.

To return to the dating example, our true selves— the selves that are grumpy some days and messy on others, inconsiderate sometimes and selfish now and again— emerge. Morning breath, bad hair days, stomach gas, bad cooking . . . "Hey, wait a minute!" you think to yourself, "what happened?" The kitchen looks like a tornado just passed through, and any discussion about money turns into an argument. Our true selves are shocked, appalled, and what else? Disappointed. Somehow, this wasn't what we'd expected.

And so it goes. The truth is you would rather watch football on television than cuddle on the sofa. She'd rather you kept your opinions about her clothing to yourself. Meanwhile, the real world of yeast infections and diarrhea, headaches and hangovers begins to creep into the artificially perfect scenario. This isn't like the movies at all. "Where is the person I met five months ago?" you find yourself wondering. "This is not the same person."

Or is it? You're still as funny and passionate as when you first met. And she's no less the successful and poised attorney you asked out. Something has changed, yes. But it's not your partner. It's how you and your partner interact. Let's face it: wearing a tuxedo or high heels all week long is impossible. Coming up with an endless array of amusing anecdotes is exhausting. Being kind and considerate and charming is possible most of the time, but certainly there are days when this can be beyond anyone's capabilities. Life has its pressures, and when these pressures come into play, we react. We react to the pressures and, yes, to our partners.

One way of reacting is by letting down the guard, the façade . . . by just not putting forth the effort to be perfect. But what does our partner see? Obviously, someone who has morning breath, bad hair days and gas, someone who is grumpy some days and messy on others, inconsiderate sometimes and selfish now and again. In other words, someone decidedly less than perfect.

"**But I was attracted to the perfect**," you complain. "That's what I wanted." Yeah, and so did your partner.

And so your expectations, both your own and your partner's, are not being met. This leads to frustration, stress, and something we talked about previously: an **ego bruise**. Sure, this is a personal situation, and our earlier reference was to a professional one (recall Jones). But the two are similar. **You have expectations. They aren't met. You feel rotten**.

In the work world, whether you are in the insurance business, high finance, education, or the restaurant business, certain aspects of your experience are similar.

The classic example is, of course, the case of the promotion.

Remember Jones? His career feels like a disaster. Having put the past behind him, he is diligently attempting, one more time, to earn the coveted promotion. This time he actually gets it. Needless to say, there is much happiness in the Jones household once this takes place. Initially, Jones absolutely revels in the luxury of his newly acquired cubicle, in his new chair, in his shiny new desk. Why, he revels in everything! Even the paper clips and rubber bands thrill him. He has arrived. He has managed to end up exactly where he wanted to be.

The problem is that before long the thrill of those paper clips begins to wear off, Jones starts to notice that this new position requires a lot more meetings than he'd anticipated. Worse still, the meetings drag on forever and he sometimes doesn't get home until nearly eight o'clock or later. He begins to notice that he can't duck out of work on sultry summer afternoons, can't make his daughter's dance recital, and can't go to see his son's baseball games. Wait! This isn't what he'd expected at all.

Meanwhile, back at home, it turns out that his wife, Mrs. Jones, has been promoted at her job. Now she has no time to make dinner or to listen to him tell her about the latest office antics. She's too tired to be patient, and she's out of town sometimes. That leaves him home alone with the kids night after night and facing dinners of microwaved fish sticks. This is even further from what he'd expected. How could something he'd wanted so badly turn out to be such a huge disappointment?

To put this another way, Jones got what he wanted, just as the dating couple—at least at the beginning—got what they'd wanted. But, it turns out that **there is a price to getting what we want**. We get to live with the reality that what we thought we wanted comes with some **unexpected extras**: bad hair days, long meetings, and more. In some ways, it seems ridiculous to describe this. After all, even as you read this, you realize that this is the texture of everyday life; over time, we see that things aren't as perfect as we sometimes hope they will be. You realize that it's natural to have to come face-to-face with the disequilibrium between formal and informal behavior. Certainly, you don't need to be told that in family situations informal behavior is the norm, whereas in formal settings formal behavior takes precedence. So, why do we feel so disappointed when our dates turn out to be normal people, or when our boss puts business ahead of our feelings? Why don't we just take a mature look at the situation and focus on the gains of the new situation? The answer? By now you know it by heart. Because we're **disappointed**. Because we let our fantasies about the future overlap with our realistic assessment of the direction things might take. Unhappy and unfulfilled, we decide we need our partners to change, our bosses to quit, our rewards to improve. But this goes nowhere. And part of the reason is that our operating presumptions in these cases led us to expect that nothing would happen, that nothing would change.

A while ago we discussed the ego bruise that often accompanies the realization that something we thought (expected, hoped?) would happen had not happened and will not happen. We discussed how those hopes and expectations may have set us up for a fall. But equally dangerous are those situations when we hope/expect that nothing will happen, that nothing will change, especially when in most situations **change is preordained**.

A friend of mine married a sexy, vivacious woman, only to find, three kids and 15 years later, that her priorities have changed . . . as has her energy level. Another friend married a nice guy who always makes a point of taking the afternoon off to attend the recitals of their three-year-old daughter's dance class. Seven years and two promotions later, my friend is on the verge of filing for divorce because this same nice guy now seems more married to his career than he is to her. Worse still, he not only never takes afternoons off any more, but often works weekends and is out of town 15 days a month on business. Meanwhile, the couple that was so infatuated with one another's formal behavior and formalized selves now learn that the other person is merely human, after all. He or she is prone to sinus infections or yeast infections. He or she gets gas when they eat cucumbers, diarrhea when they eat mushrooms. His or her at-home apparel of choice is sloppy old sweatpants; he steals the sheets and her feet stink. How awful!

Good ol' Jones, meanwhile, is shocked and appalled all over again to find that his new promotion and his wife's new job situation have robbed them of much of the freedom they used to take for granted.

What is happening in these situations? I would suggest that the various **ego bruises** experienced by the people in these illustrations are the result of an unmet operating presumption that nothing would change, that what they liked best about a given situation would go unaltered by time, new responsibilities, age or familiarity.

And so we see that one of the most dangerous psychic and emotional landmines over which we can trip is the **operating presumption**. Operating presumptions make us expect things, which may not be ours to rightfully expect in the first place; they lead us to think that the best of any given situation will never change. They lead us to ignore recognition when we're focused on reward, and to place our faith in outcomes over which we have no control. They lead us to overlook and discount the good in a given situation because we are busily focusing on the good that might have characterized that situation sometime in the past. In other words, they almost always set us up for a fall.

And yet, many of us, most of us, you and I, all still carry these operating presumptions with us over and over, week in and week out, in situation after situation. And then we wonder why we are so often disappointed. Why is it so hard for us to ask ourselves if maybe our expectations were unrealistic? Why is it so hard to accept that **we cannot control that which we don't control**? Why is it so hard to stop always wanting and expecting more?

DON'T YOU JUST LOVE A FORMAL GARDEN?

Exercise:

To anchor this teaching point, let's use a real life example. Please define an **Ego Bruise** you experienced and <u>work</u> to see if you can define the **why** and **where** it came from. Start at the top and work toward the bottom.

EGO BRUISE—How were you bruised? (*Ex: Felt rejected.*)

What was it based on?   Operating Fantasy, Operating Assumption **or** Operating Presumption?

SITUATION THAT WAS UNMET?—Defined in your real life. (My *overtures for a WILD night.*)

EXPECTATIONS:

Operating Presumption—the gray foggy area—a mixture of fact and fancy—reward or further benefit. (*Geez, I made dinner with no reward.*)

Operating Assumption—based on probability—recognition. *(If I did this, and we ARE married.)*

Operating Fantasy—set of expectancies we believe to be true. *(I'm home early, and make an effort.)*

CHAPTER 4

Truth and Lies

ða ða ða

When we were kids, one of the earliest lessons our parents and teachers tried to drum into us was the concept of truth. **We should always**, we were taught, **tell the truth**; we should not lie. But as kids, this was often a difficult lesson for us to learn, accept and take to heart. For one thing, even as little children we recognized that telling the truth would often expose us to the consequences of our actions. And even as little children, perhaps especially as little children, we wanted to be spared of those consequences as much as possible.

But slowly, over time, grudgingly and haltingly, we learned to tell the truth. Part of this was due to the realization that, just as other people looked to us for the truth, we too wanted to be able to believe what others told us. We quickly learned that if everyone lied as a matter of course, the world would be an unsettled, unreliable place. **We learned the value of the truth**. Everyone, we now accepted, should tell the truth.

Unfortunately, this is an ideal, and this we also learned as we grew. We began to recognize that people—

our parents, our friends, our bosses and even our lovers—often shaded the truth, stretched it, bent it or twisted it altogether. We began to realize that sometimes, to spare another's feelings, for example, the **truth** did not necessarily need to be told in its **entirety** . . . if at all. We began to understand the concepts of the fib and the white lie. And we also came to understand, particularly as we entered the adult **professional world**, that there were times when we were **expected to lie**.

Because the reality is that one cannot, in fact, be completely honest in real life. **In fact, one characteristic of "good manners" is, well, lying.**

❧ ❧ ❧

All of us have been trained to lie to one degree or another.   When Great-Aunt Maud shows up for Thanksgiving dinner with yet another of her cement and molasses fruitcakes, this training reminds us not to groan and tell her that everyone in the family positively hates the cakes. When the Boss tells one of his typically badly delivered, dumb jokes, this training kicks in and reminds us to at least grin, if we can't muster a chuckle. The examples are endless.

There is a hilarious scene in the movie *East is East*, for example, which illustrates this to comic effect. The male members of two immigrant families are meeting to arrange the double engagement of one family's sons to the other family's daughters. The father of the girls produces a large portrait of the two brides-to-be, unwraps it, and passes it around for the inspection of the boys' male relatives. The boys' father's eyes go wide; he purses his lips and nods. He passes the picture among his brothers, cousins, and advisors. Their reactions, with some of them murmuring, are the same. At last, the camera pans down to the portrait and we see the girls for the first time. They are positively horrid! "Beautiful," the boys' father says as he passes the picture back to those negotiating on behalf of the girls. "**You must be proud.**"

We laugh (and squirm more than a little) to see the boys' father trapped by honor and social convention. We know the girls are ugly. He knows the girls are ugly. The girls' father and male relatives all know the girls are ugly. The intended grooms will certainly know the girls are ugly when they see them. But **honor and social convention** demand that this obvious fact cannot be recognized or mentioned. It is the *Emperor's New Clothes* all over again.

"Yeah, cute, Mark," you might say, "but that's just a movie."

Yes, it is a movie, but it contains a lesson nonetheless.

Let's take another example. When you run into an old colleague on the street (not a personal friend, but simply someone you know or have worked with in the past) there is a specific routine to your interaction. He or she asks how you are. You lie and say, "Wonderful." You don't say that your spouse has just run off with an aerobics instructor of the same sex, that your son came home last evening with his lips pierced in seven places, that your 13-year-old daughter has run off with a grunge band, or that your Chihuahua has nasal tumors. You **hide** these things in favor of what social convention calls upon you to say.

In similar fashion, he or she does not divulge that his or her spouse has recently been indicted for embezzlement, that his or her eldest child has turned up as a revolutionary in the jungles of Peru, or that he or she is about to go bankrupt. Instead, you both lie; make arrangements for his or her people to call your people, and you promise to "**do lunch**."

These examples are, admittedly, somewhat exaggerated to make a point. But they illustrate the fact that we do not let this acquaintance know the truth. We don't admit that the daily stresses of work and family are taking their toll on us. We don't admit that things are not going well. We don't admit that sometimes, lately, we've been a bit depressed. **We lie**.

Or, take the opposite example as an illustration. Have you ever run into an acquaintance and asked, "How are you?" only to have this person pour out a story of tragedy, cruel fate and misfortune? Perhaps she has been divorced since you last saw her. Maybe he was fired and has been unemployed since you last spoke. Maybe there was a tragic death in the family. Whatever the bad news this person has to share, have you not had the feeling that you were **sorry you asked**, sorry you even ran into him or her? Have you not, in these circumstances, felt a bit like squirming and a lot like leaving? "Why," you probably wondered, "is he or she telling me all this?" Well you asked didn't you?

"Yeah, but I didn't really want or need to know all that stuff," you might say. "I was just being polite."

Ah, polite . . . as opposed to what? Probably, as opposed to really caring.

Now, this little example is not meant to make you feel calloused or uncaring. Rather, it is intended to illustrate how all of us, you, me and the other guy, are not only all **trained to lie** to cover up our true feelings, but we also expect that all but those closest to us will do the same.

And it isn't as simple as saving face, either. Sure,

when we're the one asked, "So, how are things?" we want the acquaintance to see us in our best light; but there's more to it than that. Certain very real defensive mechanisms are at work. Another example will make this more apparent. Imagine running into the Boss. After gently correcting him for what seems like the 700th time when he calls you by the wrong name, you assure him that everything is just fine when he asks, "So, how are things?" brushing past you in an unrepentant cloud of cigar smoke. You certainly don't tell him that your spouse has just run off with an aerobics instructor of the same sex, that your son came home last evening with his lips pierced in seven places, that your 13-year-old daughter has run off with a grunge band, or that your Chihuahua has nasal tumors. You similarly **don't tell** him that your immediate supervisor, his son, is a complete idiot who couldn't find his way out of the men's room unattended, that the promotion he recently gave to his mistress' nephew will cost the firm millions because the lad is a moron, or that your failure to get a raise over a half a percent for the past five years means that you can't pay for your cat's orthodontia. Once again, you lie. Everything's fine, you assure him as he disappears down the hall saying, "Good, good. Keep up the good work."

Somehow getting through the rest of the day, you return home, which by the way, is empty because your spouse has just run off, your son is having his lips pierced yet again, your 13-year-old daughter is in Brazil with the grunge band, and the Chihuahua has gone to Mexico for holistic treatment of its nasal tumors. Then your mother calls and asks how everything is. **"Okay,"** you say, because after all, why should you say anything that would make your mother worry?

What's going on here? The answer is this: **nothing and everything**.

The nothing is that you have not done anything abnormal or problematic. Instead, you did exactly what social convention demands of you. You haven't rocked the boat. You haven't told anyone your life is falling apart. You haven't told the Boss how you really feel about his management decisions. You haven't called attention to yourself (after all, that would be rude).

The everything is the fact that behind your lies about the life you are leading is the truth about what you're experiencing. Your family is in turmoil. You have expectations that aren't being met. You're facing crises of a personal or financial nature. Sometimes, you just want to **SCREAM!**

But when we're faced with situations like these, we can't say that . . . and we certainly can't scream.

Now, sometimes, this just goes with the turf. As a parent, for example, it would be wrong to complain to your kids, or in front of your kids, that their presence means a complete lack of privacy for you and your spouse. That lack of privacy, that lack of freedom, is one of the sacrifices that goes along with being a parent; it goes with the turf. Similarly, it would be wrong and hurtful, if we had an aged, infirm or sick parent who needed our help, to complain to that person that his or her needs were an inconvenience. Sometimes we all have to do things we don't particularly want to do and we just have to **shut up** about it. Is it a lie to hide our true feelings in these cases? Strictly speaking, probably. But it is a lie for a good cause. Without such lies, we'd probably have difficulty maintaining any close, personal relationships.

But in the larger world in which we live and operate, the lies, half-truths and omissions we utter almost every day say much about our expectations of ourselves and those that others have of us. In the examples of the brief conversations with the Boss or the acquaintance who asks how we are, for example, the truth is that, basically, the lives we are living are the exact opposite of those we described.

But why? Why is it the expected norm that we will keep our frustrations to ourselves? And why is this important?

Because it is easier, I'll answer the second question first.

This is important because such social lying not only exacerbates the stress of the situation we are masking, but produces stress in and of itself. We know, for example, that lying causes measurable changes in the body; this is the basis of the lie detector test. Why should anyone think, therefore, that the same act would not cause mental and emotional stress in our everyday lives?

"Now just hold on there a second, Mark," I can hear you objecting. "Sure, some criminal strapped to a lie detector is going to feel stress as he tries to cover up what he's done. But how can you equate that to my wanting to keep certain things private?"

It is not the desire for privacy that is at issue here. Wanting to keep certain things private is completely understandable. There is certain information, deeply personal, that we all keep to ourselves. But it is not that information that we're talking about.

Think for a moment of ongoing situations that could cause someone stress. Perhaps someone we know has a marriage that is going down the tubes and seriously suspects his or her spouse of having an affair. Perhaps his or her business is on the verge of failure and bankruptcy is looming just around the corner. Maybe the problem is a son who was just caught buying drugs in school or a 16 year-old daughter who has gotten pregnant. Maybe this person was just informed that within two weeks he or she would be fired. The examples are endless.

Now think of the stress that person probably experiences from any one of these circumstances. We can all relate, because none of us would want to face those situations. We all realize the stress any one of these situations would cause.

But now think about how that person might handle these crises. He or she would almost certainly want to hide these facts from bosses and co-workers. He or she might want to hide these facts from parents, siblings, and all but the closest friends. The situations are embarrassing. And the embarrassment, the grief, and perhaps the attendant sense of responsibility and failure in each of these situations causes stress. But, at the same time, the need, whether actual or simply perceived, to hide these truths in itself is a cause of stress. The person has to watch what he or she says, put on a façade of bravado and good cheer. He or she has to hide, at least for the moment, what he or she is truly feeling and experiencing. This effort, this need to mask the truth, causes more stress.

Further, it is not fair to say that only you or I are forced into such a situation, that the rest of the world is hard-boiled or uncaring. Remember the example we cited above, where you or I run into someone, ask how he or she is, and get unexpectedly overwhelmed with a tale of woe? Remember the discomfort we described? The truth is that each of us is **guilty** of wanting others to keep their troubles to themselves: the Boss doesn't want to hear your troubles or mine, and neither you nor I particularly want to hear the sad stories that the receptionist might have to tell.

And so we are examining this issue because it is something we all face in life. We are all called upon, largely by social convention but sometimes out of personal impulse, to **hide** much of what we experience and feel. And an essential step in understanding this and the impact it has on our lives is to understand why it is so, to understand why the **social lie** is so central a part of our lives.

CHAPTER 5

Big Girls Don't Cry

ૐ ૐ ૐ

Nor, for that matter, do big boys. And that is one of the most basic lessons behind the social lies that cause us so much stress and that are so much a part of our lives.

Are you a parent or a stepparent? Have you ever been a parent? Do you at least remember ever being a kid? If so, you must remember some time, some place where either you told a youngster, or were told yourself, that **crying was not an answer**. Admittedly, that's not such bad advice. Learning to stop blubbering about negative situations and coming up with solutions instead is the trademark of a mature response to a negative situation. But this lesson should not be confused with the all-too-human reaction of crying in reaction to intense emotional or physical pain.

When a spouse, parent or a child is hurt or dies, when the love of our life suddenly leaves, when we fall and break a leg, even when we watch the sappy ending to a romantic movie, our hard-wired response is to cry. It is a typical and involuntary reaction, well beyond our active control.

Indeed, studies have shown that individuals who are largely (or entirely) immune to this response are suffering from a severe emotional deficiency, one that is often associated with an inability to differentiate between right and wrong, to empathize with others and to comprehend and/or appreciate the results of impulse reaction. So, aspirations to **Vulcanesque** control of all emotions aside, we must accept that certain physical manifestations of physical and/or emotional pain—in this case, crying—are part of our common make-up as a species.

But beyond this, we also recognize that children cry more frequently and usually in response to less significant stimuli than do adults, or even adolescents. Several dynamics are at play here.

Children lack an adult's sense of perspective. Children cry about a skinned knee, where an adult might just swear. Younger children cry at the disappointment of a missed birthday party; older kids sulk in the face of a similar disappointment. Young children cry when their feelings are hurt, when they are taunted or teased. They cry, "No fair!" at a host of life's slights and injustices.

As adults, we, too, feel the sting of slights and injustices. We, too (internally anyway), wince at taunt or insult. But we don't cry; we don't throw a tantrum. We have learned perspective, a sense of proportion that allows us to put the incident in its proper place. This is one of the lessons of growing up.

But we have also learned something else.

Distinguishing major from minor negative stimuli and placing these stimuli in perspective is a major step on the road to maturity, true. The problem is that most of us have a sort of internal filter that continually informs us that much of whatever is bothering us isn't really important; that it's minor, or at least that is how our concerns will be seen by others. This is one of the two major sources of the stressful social lie.

To illustrate, imagine your sump pump stops working sometime in the night during a particularly heavy rainstorm. No one in the family realizes this, as you all get ready to leave the house for school or work. But at 8:10 a.m., your daughter goes down to the fully finished family room in the basement and discovers that everything down there, from her bookshelf to your brand-new Surround Sound stereo and the large screen TV system, is awash in about three inches of water. Are you upset? Of course you are.

Now it's 8:13 a.m. and you have to leave for work. Frantic, you call a plumber or two, get an answering machine or two, quickly determine that your wife can't possibly stay home from work, take one last look at your videotapes breaststroking their way past the bottom of the stairs and begrudgingly leave for work yourself.

Sometime later at work, as you are still frantically trying to reach a plumber, the Boss wanders by. After calling you by the wrong name for the 701st time now, he asks how you are. Completely obsessed by the watery situation you left at home, you mention that you have a flooded basement and are about to lose thousands of dollars in family belongings to the quickly rising waters.

Now, the Boss is an old-fashioned guy. He still thinks cigars in the office, triple bourbons at lunch, and strippers popping out of a cake at a sales meeting are all perfectly fine ways of doing business. His wife never held a job and he has no patience for the family scheduling problems of two-career households. At the mention of your flooded basement, the Boss freezes. A cold look comes over his face as he turns to suggest that your wife should be attending to the floodwaters. Realizing your mistake, you retreat, mumbling something about your wife's job.

"**Well, it sounds like a personal problem**," he responds, letting you know that he expects that come Hell or high water, no flood in the basement is going to distract you from your all-important duties at work. In other words, the Boss has drawn a line between **what you think is important and what he thinks is important**. You are expected to exercise control over your emotions (in this case, your frantic worry over the thousands of dollars worth of belongings going down for the third time in your basement) and to return your full attentions to the all-important requirements of the Firm.

So, what are you feeling? At this point we can guess that you are experiencing several **ego bruises**. Fate has flooded your basement, disturbing your notion of how things generally should go. Your wife's announcement that her presentation is too important to miss suggests she views her outside-of-the home duties as more pressing than the flood, thereby offending your archaic sensibilities. Finally, the Boss has just blown off all your concerns by announcing that yours is a personal problem, unimportant in the real scheme of things and certainly nothing that should get in the way of a full day's work. Worse still, part of you agrees with him.

And so, you feel a **conflict** with fate (the flooded basement), with your wife (because she would not stay home and deal with the flood), with your Boss (who thinks that the flood is not all that important), and with yourself (because you are torn between duty to home and a sense of duty to your job). No wonder you're frustrated!

Part of what you're feeling in all this is a specific conflict that most of us usually overlook. It is a battle between **nature and nurture**, between the way you are made and the way you were raised, between what you feel and what you believe. It is the same conflict that moves you to lie when an acquaintance asks how you are and you cover up all the troubles in your life. It is the conflict of the social lie.

What is the difference between nature and nurture, between the way you are made and the way you were raised, between what you feel and what you believe? For an answer, let's consider *Star Trek*'s **Mr. Spock**.

In Star Trek, Mr. Spock is popular, in part, because, surrounded by two-dimensional characters, he embodies a truly universal conflict in our society: **the conflict between emotion and logic**. As viewers, we admired his Vulcan emotional control, finding in that philosophy something foreign, yes, but strangely appealing. Sure, we looked hard for a crack in that facade, a touch of warmth, a smile, perhaps even a hint of romantic attraction. But why? Perhaps it was because we recognized in the character of Mr. Spock something we recognize in ourselves: a conflict. In our case, it is not the conflict between emotion and logic, per se, but the conflict between **the way we are made and the way we are raised**. There is nothing new about this conflict. Civilized humankind has been battling this conflict for more than 2000 years.

In order to understand this conflict, to understand the tug of emotions we feel when we are faced with a choice between making that important meeting or attending our seven-year-old daughter's after-school dance recital, when the choice before us is staying home to tend to our flooded basement or going to the office—to understand why we feel constantly pressured by these choices—we must understand the root of the problem.

Nature built us, wired us a certain way. We are

wired to respond with a sense of attraction and protectiveness at the sight and sound of young children; indeed, we respond this way to most young mammals, whether they are puppies, kittens or small children. Our hardwired response in these cases is to protect, to nurture. There is little logic in wanting to take in a stray kitten, but the point is that many of us, perhaps most of us, find the kitten (or puppy) in some way appealing; we want to take the kitten home. We feel moved or at least tempted to try.

Similarly, we enjoy romantic comedies, cheer when the Terminator takes out the bad guy and get a lump in our throat when our children go off to school for the first time. Again, we are wired that way, to respond to both physical and emotional pain and pleasure.

Along these same lines, we have needs, wants, and desires. But, if we all acted upon what we perceived as these needs, wants, and desires without constraint, the result would be chaos.

Upon reading the next few pages, you may think that I've gotten lost or that you've picked up the wrong book. You may wonder where I'm going with the discussion that follows. But let me assure you, there's a point to it.

You see, as I said, I want to explore the conflict between what we often **feel** and what we often **believe**, between what we feel we want to do and what we have been taught we should do, the concept I call the *social lie*. We have been discussing some of the sources of our feelings. But they are internal and the fact is that we live in an **external world**. Unless we completely understand the impact that external world has upon us, we can never truly understand much of what we experience in everyday life.

In her book *The Anatomy of Love*, Helen Fisher

touches upon one aspect of this issue when she examines the impulse to stray versus the social value placed upon marital fidelity. While I am paraphrasing here, essentially what Fisher argues is that nature wired us to spread our genes amongst the widest possible pool of attractive genes in others. For this reason, she suggests, earliest humans did not mate for life. Rather, there was a built-in impulse to mate with as many members of the opposite sex as possible to give one's own genes the greatest chance of surviving and being passed on. Against this as civilization developed, however, was the evolving social norm of fidelity and, at least in the Western, Judeo-Christian world, monogamy. Marriage and fidelity, she essentially suggests, go against the essence of how nature wired us, shaped us, and moves us. This is but one facet of the conflict between what we feel and what we are taught to believe. Fisher discusses in great length the development of the legal, social, and religious notions of marriage and fidelity.

But for the broader picture, to understand how the type of conflict Fisher points to has an impact upon our everyday lives and the myriad situations in which we find ourselves, it is necessary to go beyond her focus and look at the wider pallet of cultural norms under which we operate. Remember, **we are all born with feelings**. Even the youngest child will laugh, cry, and express desire and preference. We are not born, however, with **beliefs or values**. Those are external, learned. Therefore, to really understand both sides of the equation, it is necessary to appreciate exactly where these beliefs and values come from.

What beliefs? Well why don't we begin with the basic concepts of good and bad and proper behavior. Where did these notions come from?

Now, much of what I am about to say is particularly American in thought and context. But I am an American and I am writing to an almost exclusively American audience. Remember, we are exploring why we experience a **conflict between what we feel and what we believe**, particularly what we believe about the way we should act. Therefore, if we accept the idea that our beliefs are learned, we have to accept the fact that what we learned as Americans, living in modern American society and brought up with American values, may very well differ from what people growing up in Japan, Syria or Mexico may have learned. In other words, a good deal of what we experience as a conflict in our society and our setting may not be a conflict at all to people in other cultures. So to understand the conflict, we have to understand the culture.

Human beings have needs, wants, and desires. This is nothing new and has been a recognized fact since the dawn of civilization. But civilization implies a balance between our needs, wants, and desires and those of everyone else. The needs of the many outweigh the needs of the one—or so we have been told. Civilization mandates a set of rules, and so, if we are to understand the impact of civilization or society upon us, we have to examine the origin of those rules.

We say we live in Western society. That means the foundational norms upon which our society is built are Western, as opposed to Eastern or Oriental norms. Our most basic social values came to us from the Greco-Roman world of 2000 to 3000 years ago. For the Greeks, and for the Romans who followed them, **self-control** was considered the highest form of goodness; in fact, it was the uppermost goal of most popular philosophies of the time. With the world spinning around madly outside of the person, and needs, wants, and desires equally stirred up within a person, self control, or acting properly, came to be seen as a **virtue**. The Greeks referred to these needs, wants, and desires as passions, and they were not regarded as something to be particularly proud of. Rather, the superior person was believed to be the man or woman who exercised self-control. Such self-control was seen as a mark of excellence by which one could judge another's character, education, virtue, composure, integrity, and self-esteem (Mack, 1995). For the Greeks, self-control was the same as controlling one's passions. For them, acting civilized on the outside was more important than being civilized on the inside. If anything, they assumed that if one **acted properly**, one could not help but **think properly**.

By the time of the Romans, a person who exhibited duty and proper behavior was seen as being a perfect, law-abiding subject to Caesar. It is from this that we inherited many of our notions of honor, duty, and responsibility.

But while we say we live in a Western society, we also claim to adhere to a so-called Judeo-Christian ethic. What does that mean and how does it impact us today?

While the ancient Greeks (and later the Romans) focused on a person's living as part of society, emphasizing his or her external behavior, the ancient Hebrews were much more interested in a person's internal behavior, or what we would today call **ethics**. Thus, while the Greeks and Romans preached obeying the law ("rendering unto Caesar what is Caesar's"), the Hebrews, who were around far earlier than either the Greeks or the Romans, preached concern and regard for the feelings, needs, and desires of others. Following a law they considered to be higher than that of Caesar's, the Hebrews took very seriously the matter of social need. For them, the passions of outward self-interest that so concerned the Greeks were less dangerous than the inward passions of selfishness. We might say that, for the Hebrews, to think and feel properly would naturally lead to proper outward actions.

For centuries, these two world-views, along with those of other ancient societies that came and went, carried on side by side, each aware of, but not particularly impressed with, the other. Then came St. Paul.

Paul was a Hebrew, a Jew, who had converted to Christianity and was preaching to the Greeks—and those influenced by Greek culture—in the Roman Empire of the first century. Talk about conflict!

Paul merged the two concepts we just discussed into one new concept. He preached that the passions that should be controlled were not only the Greek externals of self-interest, a desire for advancement, goods, and station, but also the Hebrew internal concerns of physical lust, revenge, and jealousy. Paul contrasted sin and righteousness, flesh versus spirit in the same way the Greeks contrasted enslavement to the passions with self-control.

As Christianity spread in the Western world, this Judeo-Christian ethic became seamlessly grafted onto earlier notions of right and wrong, good and evil, honor and shame.

These concepts were our ancient inheritance and form much of the basis of what we consider as morality today. But just as we are products of Western thought and a Judeo-Christian ethic, we are also products of what evolved as Anglo-Saxon society.

Fast forward to the early 1600s.

By the time the Reformation had fully taken root in Europe, particularly in northern Europe, two strains of thought predominated. The first, purely theological, was a reaction to what were seen as doctrinal errors in the Catholic Church and its excesses. Many early Protestant denominations, therefore, adopted a liturgy that was plainer, simpler, and closer to the people. But an even more radical train of thought was developing in the theology of John Calvin and the English Puritans. This was a theology that rejected all excesses, and further, one that saw such excesses not just in the pageant of the Roman Catholic liturgy, but virtually everywhere else in life. For this group, colorful dress was to be shunned in favor of basic black. Singing, dancing, frivolity—in short, plain human enjoyment—were all to be shunned. Similarly, outward displays of emotion, whether of love, self-indulgent excesses or sexuality, were shunned as well. The ethic was to be hard-working, nose-to-the-grindstone types with no distractions. This was far more than the accepted way to behave. It was the way to **Heaven**.

As those of you who remember your history will recall, the **Puritans** are the people we today refer to as the **Pilgrims**. This is the group responsible for bringing these notions to the New World, to America and, ultimately, to us.

While it would be a terribly broad, reductive overstatement to say that all immigrants to the New World carried these concepts out in their daily lives, these concepts did come to represent something of an American ideal. This Protestant work ethic, this discomfort with emotionalism, the shunning of overly expressive behavior became the underpinnings of much of what we consider to be proper social behavior today.

When American society adopted the values of Victorian England, we added yet another layer to all this. In the late 1800s, Britannia ruled the waves. England was the most powerful and easily the most prestigious nation in the world. And while the French may have scoffed and the Russians blustered, here in America we still suffered separation anxiety where the Mother Country was concerned. The result was an adoption, almost a fawning imitation, of nearly everything British, their social, moral, and business code in particular.

Victorians took the Puritan work ethic, re-emphasized at least the outward appearance of Judeo-Christian social and sexual morality, stiffened it with a strict code of social behavior, and presented it as God, Queen and Country. The stiff upper lip of Gunga Din, the glorious suicide of the Charge of the Light Brigade, cries of "Women and Children First!" as the Titanic sank, were all hallmarks of this expected social behavior. Men did not cry (and real men didn't complain). A woman's place was in the home. Act properly and you'll do properly. These were the watchwords of proper British society.

And we in America bought into all of it.

So, while the French and Italians enjoyed their sexual farces on stage, shrugged at incompetent public officials, and raised hardly an eyebrow at anyone's having a mistress, while they doted on their children and lived largely for today, we (and the Germans) followed the repressed British lead into the 20th century. And where are we now?

To recap, **the Greeks wanted to control man's outer behavior; the Hebrews were concerned with controlling his inner behavior. St. Paul combined the two and effectively said all self-interested impulses needed to be controlled. The Puritans taught that this control must extend to outward signs of enjoyment and pleasure. The Victorians upped the ante, stating outward signs of discomfort and pain should be similarly suppressed.**

The only problem was—and the problem remains—that we are human beings. We are hard-wired with both negative and positive emotions. We can have, and do have, selfless impulses; but we also still have selfish ones as well. In other words, our **natural impulses** have not really changed in 5000 years. We still anger, lust, resent, and thirst for revenge. We still covet and crave. We still want a more physically comfortable life. We still get jealous. And, as Helen Fisher reminds us, we still feel an impulse to stray.

We still react positively to beauty, often not seeing the ugliness it masks; and we usually react negatively to the ugly, often ignoring the goodness it hides. We still react positively to the pleasant and negatively to the burdensome or unpleasant.

But, at the same time we also have thousands of years of accumulated acculturation telling us to deny those emotions and impulses. We are taught not to steal, not to rape, certainly not to kill. We are taught that we must obey the rules of the game and a rule or law with which we sometimes heartily disagree. We are taught to be graceful losers and gracious winners. We're taught that crime doesn't pay and that cheaters never prosper, in spite of ample evidence to the contrary. We are taught to wish the other fellow well, even as we try to beat him out of the prize. We are taught to spare the feelings of others, to act in a civil manner and leave unspoken the way we really might feel about a situation. **We are taught to be polite; we are taught to lie.**

Put another way, we have spent the better part of 3000 years as a species trying to deny our very nature as a species. The clash between what we are still hard-wired to feel and the way we've been taught to act is a conflict. We can't help it. We experience emotional pain and an ego bruise when we tell the Boss that our basement is flooded and he replies, "That sounds like a personal problem."

We experience a conflict when the other person gets the promotion and we have to congratulate her. We experience a conflict when someone says something unkind about us or does something unfair or downright nasty. That much is clear.

What can be less clear, perhaps, is the second, often exacerbating conflict we experience when we have to work under the person we feel unfairly got the promotion, when circumstances force us to bite our tongues and not reply to the unkind or nasty thing that was done to us. We experience a conflict when we have to accept the Boss' word as law and let our soggy belongings in the flooded basement just go on floating because there is work to be done at the office. We experience this conflict when we are forced, day in and day out, to live a series of social lies to act one way when we feel another.

Have you ever had the occasion to find yourself in an unexpected argument with someone, perhaps a spouse or significant other, in a public place? Have you ever had that person tell you, "**Not here; not now**"? Isn't that often even more infuriating than what set you off in the first place? Have you ever found yourself suddenly shifting to "**Not now**? **Then WHEN**?" all but forgetting the original point of the disagreement? This is the conflict I am talking about.

In this situation you are angered by something, you have experienced some sort of ego bruise. Your instinct, your hard-wired response, is to fight back . . . hence the argument. You are giving vent to your true feelings. But, the other person, by saying "Not here; not now," is reminding you that the social norms of the situation in which you find yourselves does not allow for that sort of public spat. Rather, you are called upon to partake of the social lie that nothing is wrong when you are seething. Your reaction then, "Not now? Then WHEN?" and the accompanying sense of frustration are the result of this second conflict, the one between what you're feeling and how you are supposed to behave.

Similarly, society has deemed it incorrect to throttle the idiot who insulted you at the staff meeting or the Ladies Club meeting. Not living in the Klingon Empire, you find that you can't simply assassinate the person who got the promotion in order to advance your own career. And if you want to keep your job, you can't tell the Boss to take a flying leap while you go home and rescue your belongings from the flooded basement. And all this worsens the stress you experienced from the initial wound or ego bruise.

Because what happens if we do give in to these impulses for revenge, redress, and a recount of the votes that awarded us the short end of the stick?

The Boss might say (and would certainly think), if you give voice to this conflict, that you have stepped outside of accepted norms, that you are not controlling your inner impulses. And frankly, it doesn't matter to him whether it is your impulse to stay home with your sick six-year-old or your maddening and totally incomprehensible desire to race home to save your collection of Monkees LPs from the rising floodwaters in the basement. He simply sees it as inappropriate.

Similarly, the Board of Directors, the police and a battery of lawyers would all find it inappropriate if you throttled the idiot who insulted you at the staff meeting or assassinated the person who got the promotion you wanted.

Unfortunately, neither you nor I can **change** 3000 years of accumulated acculturation. We can't change the attitudes of the Boss. We can't change the fact that your supervisor will continue to demand face time at the office, even though there's nothing to do and no sane reason for you to stay there, missing your seven-year-old's Little League game. And nowhere but in the movies would anyone cheer if you punched the officious clod who insulted you in the nose.

Nor can we, fortunately, change the way you or I are hard-wired with feelings that make us human. For the truth is that feelings can be, and are, as much a source of pleasure to the human species as they are an encumbrance. Yes, feelings cause us to experience pain, frustration, and disappointment. But, they also allow us to experience love, tenderness, empathy, and pride in the accomplishments of others. So the problem is not the feelings themselves.

The problem is learning how to deal with the conflicts to which these feelings often lead.

CHAPTER 6

S--t Happens

≈ ≈ ≈

You need not have seen "Forrest Gump" to know which letters are missing in the first word of this chapter's title; you get the message. **S--t does happen!** In fact, a lot of things over which we have **no control** happen to us whether we like it or not. But whether you nod in **bemused agreement** or shake your head in **resigned dismay** at this fact, it is important to take a closer look at what this implies for our everyday lives.

From the Age of Antiquity, through the Age of Aquarius and into the New Age of today, people have struggled with the capricious nature of life. Why, we have wondered through the centuries, does one person have the good fortune to win the lottery and another fall prey to disaster? Why does a person decide to change his route home one day, only moments before the bridge he'd normally cross falls into the river below? Why does one person belong to a family suffering from all sorts of awful diseases, another miss an important job interview because his car broke down, and yet another person get fired for the seventh time in four years—while still others win lotteries, stay healthy, get jobs and, for all intents and purposes, live happily (it seems) ever after? Worse still, why do bad things so often happen to good people, while some bad people seem to have nothing but good luck and inexplicable good fortune?

Over the years, the human race has given all sorts of names to these quirky and sometimes fatal turns of events. We have called it **luck**; we have called it **karma**. The ancient Greeks described three fates—**Clotho, Lachesis and Atropos**—each spinning out the thread of an individual's life and fortunes at will. Similarly, for thousands of years, astrologers have **looked to the stars** for signs and portents of things to come, for warnings of misfortune and guides to good fortune. The Calvinists saw good or bad luck, success and/or failure, as signs of God's predetermined favor or wrath. In the East, these same things were seen as indications of the sort of life one lived in a previous existence. Even now, as we begin the 21st century, we still cross our fingers, avoid black cats, read our horoscopes, light candles, and murmur silent prayers, all in the mad and unsubstantiated hope that the next time **S--t happens, it won't happen to us**.

But it does happen, in spite of all we do. On a maddeningly regular basis, we miss trains, get stuck in traffic, lose our keys, have the cellar flood, the computer crash, or the VCR eat our favorite tape. People get sick and die; people, perhaps even people we know, get hurt, maimed and killed in senseless, stupid accidents. Lovers leave and families fall apart. Careers come to abrupt and unforeseen ends; businesses go belly up. Hurricanes and tornadoes level whole communities. Bad luck, it often seems, dogs us as a species.

And at the same time, some people get lucky. They win the lottery, are noticed by the CEO at just the right time, or avoid a life-threatening situation by a hair's breadth.

How to account for it all? Is there an answer?

Unfortunately, the answer is, "**No, there is no answer, no accounting for any of it**." Unfortunately, stuff, good stuff and bad stuff, just happens. Usually there is no rhyme; there is no reason. There is no particular reason why the airlines lost your luggage. There is no reason why, when two cars collide on an icy stretch of road, one lands in a snow bank and one hits a tree. It simply happens.

"But, Mark," you might object, "when I got fired because they decided to downsize the department/when that jerk in the SUV hit my car/when my wife got hurt on that poorly repaired escalator, somebody was at fault."

Well, yes and no. Someone, some person might have been the agent of what happened to you in any given circumstance, but the agent is not necessarily the cause of the misfortune. Call it luck, karma, fate, or God's design, there are just things that happen in this life . . . and there's no explaining a lot of them.

It isn't always you; **you aren't cursed**. You weren't born under an unlucky star. And God, in all probability, isn't punishing you. **Trust me**; He's got better things to do.

So why is this important? If a lot of what happens is just luck, why bother discussing it?

There's really only one reason, and it is simply this: many people, when things go wrong, when s--t happens, experience frustration, pain, shock, disappointment, or, in our terms, an **ego bruise**. They're hurt, disgusted, defeated, angry, and despondent. But, is this the appropriate response? Maybe, maybe not. Before reading on, ask yourself the following questions:

❖ If you are in a hurry, rushing to finish a report, get the kids out the door to school or make that important meeting, and your cup of coffee spills all over the place, do you get angry? At whom or at what?

❖ If the car breaks down, the lawnmower won't start or the washing machine overflows, do you feel the impulse to kick the infernal machine?

❖ If you are at some sort of dinner where they are having a drawing for prizes and everyone else seems to win something but you, do you feel disappointed?

❖ If someone you know experiences really good fortune, do you feel jealous?

❖ If you make a silly mistake, drop something and break it for example, do you get angry with yourself? How angry and does this happen frequently?

We have established that we experience an ego bruise when our various expectations, be they operating fantasies, operating presumptions or operating assumptions, go unmet. For whatever reason, our perfect pictures of life, other people (or ourselves) have failed to be matched by reality. We therefore experience **cognitive dissonance**, or an incongruity between what we believe (is, should be, or will be) and what we know the situation actually to be. An excellent example of this is found in the well-documented grief response. Along with other patterned responses to grief-producing experiences, experiences such as the sudden and unexpected death of a loved one or the sudden or equally unexpected end of a close relationship, we go through a denial phase. This is the time when we simply cannot accept that the awful event has occurred. A statement such as "I just can't believe it" may sound familiar.

Now, our logical mind knows that our parent, spouse, friend or (God forbid!) child has died. But on an emotional level, we cannot accept the finality of the event. Similarly, in a situation where a spouse or significant other suddenly announces his or her impending departure, desire for an immediate separation or divorce (or simply leaves), we know what he or she is saying, but we can't accept the fact that it's over. Instead, we cling to the futile hope that he or she will come back, that this is merely a bump in the rocky road of love, that things will return to normal. What is happening here is cognitive dissonance, the glaring **mismatch** between what we have suddenly learned to be and what we thought ought to be or would be. Thus, as our perfect picture of the world, our place in it and how it will treat us is so abruptly discombobulated, we experience an ego bruise, because our sense of self, which also includes our sense of how life will go, has been severely jarred.

However, what many of us fail to understand is that while we can recognize how a major trauma such as the loss of a loved one, a relationship or a job can produce these results, we miss completely how the everyday accidents of life actually impact us in much the same way.

Consider these examples:

❖ You're running late for an important sales presentation. Rather than getting there 15 to 20 minutes early, you'll be lucky to get there on time. Suddenly, 200 yards in front of you, a huge tractor-trailer overturns, spilling used auto parts across the road. Cars are screeching to a halt to your left, to your right, in front and in back of you. Fortunately, no one is hurt, but no one is

going anywhere either. What's your reaction?
More than likely it's "!@#%$$#%^&*(&&^
$#%#!!!). Blinkin', bleedin', son-of-a-!@#$%$#
$%^*&*^%$#@#%^%. Why does this have to
happen to **ME**?"

❖ You've been trying to get a date with Ms.
Wonderful for a while now. In a decidedly weak
moment, Ms. Wonderful accepts your invita-
tion. You shower, shave, trim your nose hairs,
and have a friend with some fashion sense pick
out your clothes. You memorize all the top
news items of the week, practice 127 witty ice-
breaking lines in case the conversation lags,
watch a PBS special or two (in case Ms.
Wonderful is of an unexpectedly intellectual
bent), buy a case of Binaca, and head out the
door—only to find that your car won't start.
What's your reaction? More than likely it's
"!@#%$$#%^&*(&&^$#%#!!!). Blinkin', bleed-
in', son-of-a-@#$%$#$%^*&*^%$#@#%^%.
Why does this have to happen to **ME**?"

❖ It's going to be that long-awaited special weekend. Your fairly new significant other, a single
parent with four kids, has finally gotten their
good-for-nothing ex-spouse to take the kids for
an entire weekend. You've got the wine on ice,
you've got the lobster tails butterflied, poached
and chilled to perfection, just waiting to be
placed on that bed of lettuce next to the caviar
you blew the month's cable payment on. You've
made the perfect fresh dill mayonnaise as a top-
ping for the lobster. The vegetables are steamed
to perfection, lightly tossed, and just awaiting
the walnut oil dressing you blew $12.98 on. The
perfectly chilled rice and scallion salad is in the
refrigerator. The music is queued on the CD

player. The lawn is trimmed, the table is set, the sheets are fresh, the scented bath oils (for two!) are ready to be poured, the movie is queued on the VCR, the flowers have just been delivered. Reservations for tomorrow's sail on the lake have just been confirmed. You await their arrival . . . here comes the car . . . you pour the champagne in eager anticipation of your date's reaction to all your efforts . . . the car is in the driveway . . . you open the door, two glasses of champagne in your hand . . . the car door is opening . . . and then you see them . . . not just his insufferable son, Junior, but Junior's sisters as well . . . all in the car. Worse still, three of them look like death warmed over and have green stuff coming out of their noses. Your (fairly new) significant other explains that within the last 18 hours three of the kids have come down with a rare sub-equatorial disease, that even though the youngest child isn't sick she didn't want to stay home for an entire weekend alone, and their parent went out of town. Finally, they say that they hope you don't mind. What's your reaction? More than likely it's !@#%$#%^&*(&^$#%!." Blinkin', bleedin', son-of-a-!@#$%$#$%^*&*^%$#@#%^%. Why does this have to happen to **ME**?"

Now while none of these things may have actually happened to you, I think you can recognize in each example the fact that, had you experienced any of them, things did not turn out the way you might have hoped. If any of them had actually happened to you, you would have been frustrated. You would have felt cheated. You would have experienced an ego bruise.

But then what?

Ah . . . now that's the important question, because depending on how you choose to interpret the event, you could either *react* or *respond*.

If we **react**, we essentially allow our emotional side to take over and the outcome will probably be a lot of energy wasted on being angry about the situation. In these cases, we look for someone or something to blame and, blame basically being an emotional justification for our feelings; we seek to rebalance the scales of justice by **venting our spleen**. We scream, yell, and perhaps toss an inanimate object or two. We sulk, pout, and generally ruin the rest of the day for ourselves and those unfortunate enough to be around us.

But, if we choose to **respond**, we have more choices. Why?

As you have noticed, I use two very different words to describe the ways in which we answer negative and positive stimuli: react and respond.

Let's start at the beginning, with the stimulus, the thing that gets all this going. A stimulus is an activating event, something that moves our subconscious brain to answer in some way. A reaction is an automatic answer to stimuli. Much the same as the way we automatically recoil without even needing to think about it if we touch something hot and burn ourselves, a reaction kicks in almost before the thinking mind considers the facts:

- ❖ We get slapped; we get mad and say, "Ouch!"

- ❖ Someone cuts us off on the Interstate; we get angry and curse.

- ❖ We learn that our significant other was seen flirting with someone else; we get mad and scream.

- ❖ We find out that the boss' brain-dead nephew

was awarded the account we were working toward; we get angry and curse.

❖ There's an accident blocking our way on the road, the car won't start or our significant other totally ruins our plans by showing up with Junior and his three sniveling sisters; we get mad and vent our spleens.

In all of these cases, the almost instantaneous result, the reaction, is to get mad, to answer what we perceive as a negative stimulus with an equally negative set of attitudes or actions. In fact, we really cannot help this fact. It is part of the way we are hard-wired, our fight or flight signal flashing in the deepest and oldest parts of our brains. The key here is to understand that the subconscious brain processes physical and emotional hurt in almost the same way: "I have been hurt!" the message registers, " I must strike back in self-defense or flee in the face of insurmountable danger!" And so, if the instantaneous mental calculus does not inform us that we're facing insurmountable danger, the instinctive reaction is to strike back, to lash out at what it was that hurt us. Sometimes that lashing out comes in the form of angry words. Sometimes it comes in the form of a non-verbal, but unmistakable display of anger, storming out of the room and slamming the door, for example. Sometimes, unfortunately, it comes out in the form of an actual physical assault. Either way, it is our *fight reaction* taking over.

But, the truth is that we also have the ability to **short-circuit** this hard-wired message and instinct, and, in fact, not react. In other words, we have the ability to **respond**.

What, then, is a response as opposed to a reaction? As I said a moment ago, a reaction issues from the deepest recesses of our instinctive sense of self, the self-preservation instinct, if you will. A **response**, on the other hand, is informed and shaped by our **thinking, analytical mind**.

This is the part of our mind that takes sources, conditions, probable intent, the outcome of our reaction/response, the bigger picture, and a host of other considerations into account.

Thus, if a stranger slaps us, we get mad and react by trying to take his or her head off. But if a child slaps us, we process the incident differently and respond rather than react, and the child's head remains intact.

What is involved here? The first is an estimation of the facts. Let me give you an example. I'm dating a woman named Linda and we are going to go to a very, very fancy French restaurant. Tonight's the night that I'm going to ask this woman to be my wife. I have a three-carat solitaire in my pocket, and I've practiced my most charming lines. I'm going to be witty, engaging, and sensitive. I dress my best, have the car washed, pick her up, and off we go. We get to the restaurant and I happen to know the maitre d'. His name is Anthony. Not Tony, mind you, but Anthony.

"Hello, Anthony."

"Hello, Mark. Hello, Linda, how are you tonight?"

"Great, wonderful, everything is fine."

"Mark, we have a little bit of a problem."

"Gee, Anthony, what's that?"

"The table you asked for hasn't turned over yet. Do you mind if I sit you at another table?"

"No problem," I say, "'cause that's the kind of guy I am."

So we sit down and the waitress comes over and with no greeting, hello or preamble of any kind, she says, "Yeah? So what do you want to drink?"

Now I'm a little bit taken aback. As I've said before, all of us go through certain rites of passage, and tonight's little rite of passage is going to be a bottle of special champagne for $140, so I've been expecting maybe a little bit more formality than I'd get ordering a beer at Ralph's.

But, undaunted ('cause that's the sort of guy I am), I turn to the waitress and say, "We'll have a bottle of Cristal." She comes back, pops the cork, pours me a glass, pours Linda a glass.

Not even pausing long enough to let us taste the champagne, she hands us menus and says, "We got three specials tonight; we got a filet of sole almandine, duck l'orange, and something to do with veal and peppers. What do you want?"

Trying to make the best of this unfolding disaster ('cause that's the sort of guy I am!) we order. The waitress disappears for about 20 minutes, then comes back and throws down the salads.

Smiling through all of this and urging the lovely Linda to ignore the waitress and focus on her salad, we begin eating. Suddenly, while I'm literally mid-munch, she shows up again and picks up the salad dishes and whisks them away.

She reappears and without so much as a word, she throws down the entrees and about nine minutes later picks them up.

Once again I smile ('cause that's still the sort of guy I am) and suggest to the still lovely, but bewildered Linda that we order dessert. The waitress wheels the dessert cart over and says, "Look, we got an apple tort, we got a raspberry tort, we got a chocolate soufflé that takes 45 minutes to prepare, which, since you didn't order it before dinner, you can't have . . . so what do you want?"

Whoa! Talk about customer service!

And when the bill comes, I do something very much out of character. I stiff her on a tip. The woman ruined my dinner, ruined the proposal I had in mind for the lovelier-than-ever Linda, and if I can't get the wheels back on this cart soon, this waitress, who I don't even know, may have ruined the rest of my life!

"Terrible service," I say, agreeing with Linda, resolving to tell my friends never to go this restaurant again. I storm out without even a good-bye nod to Anthony.

In short, I **react**.

Now, here's the same situation again. I'm still going to ask Linda to be my wife. We go to the restaurant:

"Hello, Mark. Hello, Linda."

"Hello, Anthony."

"How do you do, whadda ya say, whadda ya know?"

"We have a little bit of a problem."

"Gee Anthony, what's that?"

"Well, the table that you asked for in the Atrium hasn't turned over yet. Would you mind if we sat you at another table?"

My focus is on Linda, not on what table I'm sitting at, so I say, "Anthony, not a problem."

We sit down and the waitress comes over and says, "Yeah, what do you want to drink?"

"We'll have that bottle of Cristal," I say. And again, she comes over, pops the cork, pours me a glass, pours Linda a glass. Again not even pausing long enough to let us taste the champagne, she hands us menus and says, "We got three specials tonight; we got a filet of sole almandine, duck l'orange and something to do with veal and peppers. What do you want?"

She throws down the salads and she picks 'em up, throws down the entrees and picks 'em up, and here comes the dessert cart. And we've got that apple tort, we've got the raspberry tort, and we've got that same chocolate soufflé which takes 45 minutes—the one we didn't order before dinner so we can't have it. But, now when the bill comes I do something very different. I take the opportunity while Linda is in the ladies' room to approach Anthony.

"Was everything fine, Mark?" he asks.

"Well, Anthony, to tell you the truth, everything was not fine. That waitress—I recognize her, so I know she's not new—well, her idea of service is terrible. I mean, I don't know what's wrong with her, but I just wanted you to know. . . ."

Anthony says to me, "I'm terribly sorry, Mark. It's been a difficult situation. You see it's her first night back after six weeks. Her 17-year-old daughter and 14-year-old son were killed in a head-on car crash with a drunk driver."

"Gee Anthony, that's a very sad story. I'm sorry for her loss, but thanks for telling me."

Now, when I pay the bill, I leave her a 20 percent tip.

Did that waitress' behavior change one iota? Obviously not. The only thing that changed was the way that **I thought** about her behavior and the behavior I displayed in reply.

In the first example, I **reacted** to the little voice in my head that was screaming, "I'm a victim, I'm being abused, this waitress doesn't know what the hell she's doing . . . blah, blah, blah." In the second example, I **responded**. In that case, her behavior did not influence the way I behaved toward her or the situation. What was different?

The answer is that in the second case I had **facts** to weigh, **facts** that helped me step back, rationally analyze the situation, accept what I initially interpreted as an ego bruise and move on.

In conclusion, **facts matter** . . . and this is something I want to emphasize.

We've all heard the phrase, "**My mind is already made up. Don't confuse me with the facts.**" While we may smile at the obvious closed-mindedness the phrase makes reference to, we must also admit that it points to a sad truth. People, all of us, all too often get angry at a situation before all the facts are in. Why do we do this?

There are many reasons. In some cases, the person experiencing the anger sees a pattern in someone else's behavior, a pattern that has always caused anger before. Therefore, the injured person reacts to what he or she sees as a continuation of that pattern, whether or not the actual event truly fits into that pattern. In other cases, the facts appear too difficult to ascertain, too hard to find or too much trouble to sift through. Getting **angry is always easier**, so that's what many people do. Finally, facts can— and often do—jar preconceived notions or prejudices.

Perhaps these preconceived notions or prejudices were inherited from parents. Perhaps they came from a class or racial perspective. Either way, these preconceived notions or prejudices can make life seem simpler to some people, giving them categories into which they can pigeon-hole other people in terms of nationality, religion, class, race, activities or situations without ever having to actually think for themselves about what they're doing. These people subconsciously feel as though they have the benefit of actual experience with the targets of these preconceived notions even though they probably do not. It is therefore not at all uncommon for these people to actively avoid the facts if their prejudices are going to be seriously challenged by what they might learn. Much better, they reason, to be **happily ignorant** rather than **informed but stressed**.

But, the truth is, in spite of these examples or the people we may know who fit into any of these typologies, **facts are our friends**.

Facts tell us what really comprises a situation. Facts tell us what another person has done. Facts give us our only true guidance in the world; and facts usually help us avoid mistakes.

So, we learn that if we want to respond, rather than simply react, facts are the most basic tool we need in any situation. We can go off half-cocked in a negative situation, take things at face value, and react badly to an already bad situation—or we can step back, try to find out what other variables we have not yet seen might be in play, and then decide upon a response.

I would like to call your attention to the chart on the next page. The theme is **F.E.A.R.**, standing for False Evidence/Emotion Appearing Real. I think it fits particularly well here because, as we are talking about reacting versus responding, or using our thinking, analytical minds versus our more primitive feeling brains, the diagram illustrates how negative reactions feed upon themselves.

You know the feeling. You are stressed, and that stress causes more stress because now you are stressed about being stressed.

In these cases, the sense that we are facing over-whelming odds informs our ever-befuddled brain that we're dead meat . . . that we've got no chance . . . that we're as good as dead . . . whether or not that is actually the case. This sense (or False Evidence Appearing Real) takes over. The brain then sends out a message to the body: RED ALERT!!!!!! The body responds by leaping into its fight or flight mode, adrenaline is released, our blood pressure goes up, our heart beats faster, our mus-cles tense, our breath gets short and shallow. This leads to a physical state we call **anxiety**. We feel the anxiety, and our body reacts to it in the following way: more adrenaline is released, our blood pressure goes up even more, our heart beats even faster, our muscles tense even more, our breath gets shorter and shallower. And now, since we're already about to explode, we **panic** . . . and usually do something stupid.

But, as the model illustrates, if we **shift our strate-gy** and call our thinking minds into play, we can avoid much of this by responding rather than reacting.

So take a moment and look at the diagram on the following page. See if it doesn't illustrate this for you, and then we'll get back to our discussion. By the way, please answer the three questions at the bottom of the illustration.

F E A R
FALSE EVIDENCE APPEARING REAL

- **APPRAISAL OF *POTENTIAL* DANGER**

- **ANXIETY**
  Intense *EMOTIONAL* Reaction

- **PANIC "Cue"**

THINKING OR COGNITIVE

FEELINGS

SHIFT OUR STRATEGY

Are you a reactor or a responder?

Respond to the statement: "What is, IS."

Do you base your perceptions on facts or emotions?

Okay, so let's go back to the restaurant where I've just finished responding, rather than reacting, to the waitress' poor performance. Is there anything else this little scenario can teach us?

I think it is safe to say that the second restaurant scenario also illustrates that, along with the primary self-preservation instinct I mentioned before, we also have the capacity to **empathize**. In this case, the pain and the trauma the waitress has been going through outweighs my annoyance at the fact that my plans for a perfect, romantic dinner have been ruined . . . in other words, I gained **perspective**.

Fine. But along with this perspective, the space we carve out to consider how to answer a negative stimulus, we also need to get back to the question of whether our anger at things that happen is justified. In this case my empathy for the waitress' plight short-circuited my angry reaction to her rude service. Somewhere I was thinking, "Gee . . . if that had happened to me I don't know that I'd even be back at work. . . ." Empathy, along with the facts of the matter, told me that my anger was not justified, that it was not really her fault that my perfect night did not go perfectly and that she was probably doing the best she could.

This case was somewhat out of the ordinary because there was another side of the coin to consider. But what about when there is not another perspective that is so easy to understand? How do we react/respond then?

Simple, right? Well, it should be. Try this exercise for yourself:

ᶳᵃ ᶳᵃ ᶳᵃ

Exercise:
React or Respond?
(Please be honest when you write your answers.)

A stone flies up from a truck ahead of you and cracks your windshield . . . *React or Respond?*

Your flight at the airport is cancelled . . . *React or Respond?*

You run out of windshield washer fluid in your car, and realize this when you need it and you are going 65 mph . . . *React or Respond?*

Your train in going to be 35 minutes late . . . *React or Respond?*

You have a flat tire on your car . . . *React or Respond?*

Your date for the evening never shows . . . *React or Respond?*

You get stuck in traffic and are going to be late for the theater . . . *React or Respond?*

You just had a manicure and you chipped a nail . . . *React or Respond?*

❞ ❞ ❞

We have established that when things go wrong, when **S--t happens**, we often experience an ego bruise. I would like to take a few moments to explore the sensitive question of whether this is always appropriate.

The question is sensitive because:

1. the answer very often is "No, Dummy, you don't have a right to be angry or hurt" and
2. this is not the answer most people want to hear.

We experience **ego bruises because of cognitive dissonance**, because of the sudden mismatch between the way we expect things to go and the way they are actually going. But the first thing we should be asking is whether these expectations were reasonable in the first place.

We've already discussed operating fantasies, operating assumptions and operating presumptions. We have established the following: When the events don't match our operating fantasies or operating presumptions, it's time to take a look at the expectation itself. Because as much as we hope to blame someone or something, it may very well be the expectation that is at fault here. In other words, our expectations may have been based more on what we wanted to happen than on what was likely to happen.

I call this the "**Formula for Making Yourself Crazy**," and it goes like this:

$$\text{STRESS} \times \text{WORRY} = \text{ANXIETY} + \frac{\text{ACTION}}{\text{INACTION}} + \frac{\text{STATE}}{\text{FRENZY}} \times \text{OF} = \frac{\text{FULL-BLOWN PERSONAL}}{\text{MISERY}}$$

We all recognize how this formula fits in where our expectations, whether based on operating fantasies or operating presumptions, were unrealistic. But let's take a look at how we react or respond when our mostly valid operating assumptions go unsatisfied.

These are examples of things we have every right to expect to happen:

- When we show up for the 7:38 train, we can expect that it will be there.
- When we get on the Interstate, we can expect that our 15-minute trip will take roughly 15 minutes.
- When we get in the car and turn the key, we can expect that the car will start.
- When we turn on a light, turn on the TV, or turn on the water faucet, we can expect that light, sound and a picture, or cold water will result.

Still, we're aware that, even in situations like these, our expectations sometimes are unmet:

- The 7:38 is delayed until 8:20.
- There's an accident on the Interstate that ties up traffic for an hour.
- The car won't start.
- The light bulb burns out, the power is out, or there's a water main break down the block.

The question before us is whether these incidents merit an ego bruise. For some people, the answer is "**YES!**" These are people who simply cannot handle anything going wrong in their lives. These are people who constantly moan, "**Why me?**"

I love that question. Whenever someone asks it, I want to reply, "Why not you? You have someone better in mind?"

The truth is this question is not as supercilious as it may sound. What I'm asking is whether they are bemoaning the bad turn of luck itself, or the fact that it chose them as a target? If they are bemoaning the bad turn of luck itself, we must stop here and remind them, and ourselves for that matter, that **S--T HAPPENS!!!**

It is important to recognize that trying to figure out

the "**why**?" of every negative thing that happens in life is a negative in itself. Here are three reasons why:

1) Trying to figure out the "why?" of every negative happening is, in effect, **an attempt to gain an impossible degree of control over our environment**. The person who obsesses over why Dad suddenly died is, in reality, futilely trying to exert control over death itself. If I understand why, then I can know what I should have done, or Mom should have done, or the doctor should have done to prevent Dad from dying. **WRONG!** If Dad died suddenly of natural causes, there was probably nothing you, your mother, or the doctor could have done. You can't exert that sort of control that will prevent accidents, that will prevent the company you work for from going bankrupt, that will prevent someone close to you from suddenly taking ill. These things simply happen.

2) Very often the real goal of focusing upon the "why?" of a negative situation is to **allocate blame**. As we stated earlier, deciding who or what is to blame for something negative is an exercise in justification. But what are we trying to justify, exactly? In most cases, the answer is "**our feelings**."

   Generally speaking, we can identify several types of people when it comes to the placing of blame:

   a) **The Martyrs**. These are the folks who **blame themselves for everything**, whether or not they were actually responsible for the negative occurrence. One version of this type tends to have a bad, weak or poorly formed self-image as the basis of much of their worldview. Thus, placing blame on themselves justifies the negative sense of self by giving them further evidence of their lack of worth as human beings. Another version of this person takes the blame as a way to focus attention upon themselves instead of the actual victims. Thus the mother who says, "I should have seen it coming and done something" when her daughter's 20-year marriage dissolves in divorce is quite often a tad jealous of the attention her daughter is getting from friends and loved ones. The mother's "selfless" act in blaming herself is not only silly, it is often a sad cry for attention.

b) **The Victims**. These are the people who always **blame someone or something else** when negative things happen, even when they are at least partially responsible for whatever has occurred. These people are seeking, as we will discuss below, protection from responsibility; they simply cannot accept responsibility for themselves or for their own actions. This type of person may neglect to have the oil changed in the car for two years, but may nonetheless blame the car manufacturer for building "such a piece of junk" when the car breaks down. Or they may blame their spouse for not reminding them to get the oil changed or, better yet, having had the oil changed on their own. They will get mad at the Boss for never giving them a free minute during which they might have had the oil changed and on and on and on. These are people who miss the job interview or the big test and always come up with a reason, perhaps a faulty alarm clock or a trick knee, to justify the feeling that the lost job or the failing grade "**isn't my fault**."

c) **The Inquisitors**. The final sort of blame-seek-
er includes those who are always **absolutely
certain that someone must be at fault** whenever something bad happens, from the salt
shaker that accidentally falls out of the cup-
board and breaks the plate it lands on, to the
hot water faucet that suddenly starts drip-
ping . . . it has to be someone's fault. In many
ways, these people, too, are trying to exert
control over their entire environment. They
are the ones who are constantly shrieking,
"Who's responsible for this mess?" They often
come up with the most outlandish reasons
why it's your fault they crashed the car
('cause you asked me to run that errand), why
the linoleum wore out ('cause you kids are
always shuffling your feet while you wash
the dishes) or why the wallpaper is peeling
('cause you and the kids are always taking
steamy showers). What they are really saying
is that if they can find a way to intimidate
everyone in their lives into being **perfect** (as
they define perfect), then nothing bad will
ever happen to them again.

But whichever example we use, what we're seeing
are people who are essentially justifying their disappointment or anger, their sense of worthlessness or victimiza-
tion, by finding a place to focus **blame**.

Now, this is not to say that blame is never valid.
Sometimes there are incidents that force you to look in the
mirror and say, "**Hey, Stupid . . . you blew it**." Sometimes
there are cases when you have to point out to a child, for
example, that he did something very irresponsible by
leaving the saw out in the rain where it could rust. In
some cases, this concept carries with it a legal liability and
the result is a lawsuit.

But these are examples of where the concept of *responsibility*, much more than blame, has a proper place in the equation. This is an important distinction. Responsibility tends to be an objective measure: either the unfortunate Jones had responsibility for sending out the important package that never arrived, or he didn't. Either the child left the saw out in the rain or he didn't. Either the driver whose car hit the school bus was drunk or he wasn't. Blame, on the other hand, tends to be much more subjective. With blame, the deciding factor is not the existence of a memo clearly outlining Jones' responsibility for the package that was never sent, or the fact that the only person who took out tools happened to be the forgetful child. Rather, blame is often assigned on the basis of the opinion, largely unsubstantiated by fact, that if it had not been for the actions or request of someone else, the negative occurrence would never have taken place.

In short, the exercise of placing blame accomplishes nothing except to make us feel better by justifying something we believed or felt long before the negative incident even happened.

3) The third reason why trying to figure out the "why?" of every negative situation is itself a negative is because it **distracts us or prevents us** from dealing with the negative occurrence. As human beings, we have only so much physical, mental, and emotional energy, and the energy we spend on one thing can't be spent again on something else. Thus, in a way that closely parallels the choice between reacting and responding, we also have a choice between dealing with a negative occurrence, or becoming absorbed in trying to figure out the "why?" of it. Clearly, the more time and energy we spend on the latter,

the less time and energy we will have available
to spend on the former.

So, if we focus on the "**why**?" of a random negative
occurrence ("Oh, God. Why did the mudslide have to hit
my house? What did I do to deserve this?") or on the
placing of blame for whatever happened ("If you hadn't
accepted this damned job and made us move out to
California, we wouldn't be faced with the fact that a mudslide just destroyed our house."), we have precious little
time or energy left to deal with the negative occurrence.

It is a simple question: Which is more important?
Blaming God, ourselves or our spouse for the mudslide,
or getting about the business of picking up the pieces and
getting on with life?

Remember, the only real freedom from the capricious nature of life is death. And how many of us think
that that's the better option?

So, we have to make some **choices**. Will we learn
to live with negative occurrences in a healthy manner, or
will we choose to let them control us?

Will we react, or will we respond? The choices are
up to us.

In this chapter I have tried to deal with a subject
that, understandably, drives many people crazy: Why do
bad/inconvenient/troublesome/awful things happen,
and how should I reply to them? I have tried to suggest
that one step would be deciding whether we want our
replies to be *reactions* **or** *responses*. I have pointed out that
the reaction is usually emotionally driven, unthinking
and a lashing-out of sorts. The response, by contrast, is
driven by thought, a consideration of the facts and, where
possible, empathy.

But beyond this, I have also illustrated that focusing on the "**why**?" of every bad situation leads nowhere. Above all, placing blame, particularly upon those in no way truly responsible, is truly a dead end.

Bad things happen. **S--t happens!** **It is part of life**. We can't change it. But what we can change, at least in part, is the impact we allow these things to have on our lives and the lives of those around us . . . and one way to do that is by getting past questions of "why?" and "who's to blame?"

In the end, we have to deal with whatever bad things happen anyway, whether it is the death of someone close to us, the loss of someone's love, the loss of a job, coffee spilled on our report, a broken lawnmower or lost keys. In the end, we've got to pick up the pieces and get moving again.

So why make ourselves even more miserable by asking "why?" Why waste time?

Why not just get moving?

CHAPTER 7

You Control the Horizontal

ಶಾ ಶಾ ಶಾ

At several points in this discussion, I have mentioned control and have talked about things people try to control and things over which they have no control. Now, I want to turn to another aspect of this question of control, namely, control over daily life. This is something I want to explore because learning how control works, recognizing what we can and cannot control, recognizing the difference, and developing a strategy for exerting the control we do have are major aspects of this book.

Let's return to the disappointed daters we used as illustrations earlier. Each person was disappointed by the fact that his or her respective **operating presumptions**, much like those of the woebegone Jones, were unmet. Whether the unmet expectation was the disappointed man's presumption that the evening would continue or the disappointed woman's presumption that the first date would lead to a second date, each was an example of something over which the central actor had no *effective control*.

AND WHO'S PULLING YOUR STRINGS?

What is **effective control**? Simply put, it is the ability to make someone else do something we want them to do or, more to the point, the ability to make someone else do something they do not want to or normally would not want to do.

Getting someone to pass the salt is not effective control; that is something, which, all other things beings equal, another person would have no problem doing for us. Getting someone to pass up front row seats on the Jets' 50-yard line on a perfectly beautiful football Sunday, however, is an example of effective control. The general rule of thumb, the operating assumption in this case, is that anyone above us in the **food chain** has the potential for some degree of effective control over us. Thus, the Boss definitely has the potential for effective control. When you were young, your parents and teachers had effective control over you, or at least they should have had. If you are in the military, anyone who outranks you has effective control over you. And the list goes on.

We will examine deciding who has a right to this control, who doesn't, who uses it properly, and who doesn't in just a bit. But for now, let's keep focused on the concept of control. Certainly, we have all experienced effective control; without question, someone somewhere has exerted this type of control over us.

Put more simply, effective control is a form of motivation. Susan Butt (Author of Psychology of Sport), teaches that there are three main methods for motivating people: *aggression, neurotic conflict,* and *competence.* Let's examine these methods.

Aggression

The essence of the aggression approach is a threat of imminent or possible consequences: "Do it to them before they do it to you." "You had better do what I say, or else you're going to get it." "I'm the doctor/boss/parent and I told you to do it my way." Sound familiar? This style of motivation actually works well for some people. More passive personalities often like to be told what to do. These people see externally imposed regimentation as positive; a military setting or another strict hierarchy is appealing to them. Why?

There are several reasons. One is that the external authority figure alleviates any need for the subordinate person to make decisions and/or to accept responsibility for the results of those decisions. We can easily see how this hierarchical structure absolves a private from responsibility if a battle goes badly; the blame is aimed at the general who planned and ordered the engagement. In a working environment, the strict decision-making hierarchy is structured to both reward and punish the decision makers while generally absolving and protecting the underlings. But does this dynamic describe any of our interpersonal relationships? **Yes!**

The husband or wife who lets a spouse make all the important decisions (and often the unimportant ones as well) is an example of a person seeking protection within a clearly established domestic hierarchy. The person who, although married and with children of his or her own, still looks to his or her parents for guidance on all matters of any consequence is an example of someone who is still looking for the protection of the parent/child hierarchy of authority. It is not enough to simply characterize such a person, especially if we are married to him or her, by saying, "He/she never grew up." Rather, the key is to understand that this person is actively trying to avoid responsibility; he or she is seeking protection from consequences. He or she is looking for the protection remembered (even if only subconsciously) from childhood experiences.

But seeking this sort of protection from consequences does not have to stop at merely using another person as a shield. The person who develops a reliance on astrologers, tarot cards and fortune tellers, for example, is seeking in fate or the stars a mechanism of protection from responsibility. In other words, it is not his or her fault that failure occurred, that he or she had an affair or bet (and lost!) the mortgage in a poker game. It was fate or the stars that ordained both the action and the outcome. The individual remains **blameless**.

This is true, too, of the person who abuses alcohol or prescription drugs. Yes, there are other genetic, physical or physiological factors that can and do weigh into the equation of such dependencies. But seeking an excuse to avoid responsibility can be, and often is, an emotionally motivating factor. "**It wasn't my fault**. I was drunk." How many times have we heard that excuse offered for everything from boorish behavior to assault (on the part of both the perpetrator and the victim)? Either way, from this person's perspective, he or she is blameless.

A person who develops a physical ailment, complaint or condition that defies identification, treatment, and cure may also be seeking a similar protection from responsibility. "I can't take control of (fill in the blank) because I'm not well." This statement may often be little more than a thin disguise for the fact the person experiencing the alleged ailment is looking for a shield from the responsibilities of life.

But what about the other side of this equation? What about the person who constantly seeks to impose control over everything and everyone in his or her life? We have all heard of the alpha male, the dominant member of the pack who exerts authority and control over all other members of the group. We should recognize that in nature and in everyday life there are alpha females as well. **Alpha folks**, as we might call them, usually seek to exert an abnormal degree of control over others. Who are these people?

The list of examples is nearly endless: The Boss who consistently seeks ways, even petty ones, to demonstrate his effective control over those below him in the hierarchy, is one familiar example. The father who declares a "moratorium on peas until further notice," even though it is the only vegetable his long-suffering wife can get the kids to eat, is yet another. And even the person, who never shuts up and tries to dominate every conversation he or she is near, is an example of a person trying to exert control over all around him or her. What motivates these people?

Although there may be others, **five** possibilities come immediately to mind:

❖ The person may be motivated by an attempt to control his or her entire environment, futilely trying to structure every operating fantasy and operating presumption into an operating assumption. In other words, this person seeks, by displaying control of all those around him, to control the greater environment over which he actually has no control. An example is the person who, following some family crisis, becomes an absolute dictator or a smothering overprotector at home, exerting control over even the most insignificant aspects of household life. Put

another way, this person is seeking to compensate for his or her inability to control the larger
environment by exerting undue and abnormal
control over the immediate environment and the
people around them.

❖ The person, who, resenting the past or present
authority figures in his life, seeks subconscious
revenge, or a balancing of the scales, by exerting
undue or abnormal control over all within his
immediate sphere of influence.

❖ An individual with a weak or underdeveloped
self-image may be seeking to compensate for her
own feelings or fears of inadequacy by exerting
undue and abnormal control over her immediate environment and the people around her.

❖ A person with a weak or underdeveloped self-
image may be motivated to seek validation,
approval, and reinforcement for his weak sense
of self by exerting undue and abnormal control
over his immediate environment and the people
around him to compensate for his insecurities.

❖ The parent who just will not accept that the children have grown and continues to try to exert
control over the lives of her adult offspring may
be expressing her fear of either change or growing old, of being rendered obsolete. Often, a
poorly formed self-image, one that centers its
identity solely on the role of parent/protec-
tor/provider, is the basis of this sort of behavior.
"If I am no longer Mommy (or Daddy)," this
thinking goes, "what or who am I?" Thus, this
person seeks validation and affirmation by per-
petuating the parent/child relationship, in other
words, by exerting control.

We could, no doubt, come up with many more examples of "**control freaks**." But the point is made: these are people who habitually use **aggression** to motivate others: they take control, one way or another (aggression), to make others back down (and thereby yield control).

Neurotic Conflict

A second way to motivate people is by putting them in the position of experiencing the conflict between "**I have to . . . but I can't; I have to . . . but I don't want to . . . but I should**." Thus what we have is, "I know I have to quit smoking, but I can't quit smoking, but I have to quit smoking, but I like smoking, but I should quit smoking, but I can't, but I have to, but I can't, but I should, but I have to." We end up spinning around, never getting anywhere. Some of you may know this as either **Catholic, Jewish or Italian guilt**, except that the familiar examples in those cases usually are, "Mama wants me to do this, but I want to do that. Mama says I should do that, but I need to do this." And, let's face it, **the guilt works**! This is what we refer to as **neurotic conflict**.

Interestingly, it is exactly this tension that the Boss tries to establish when he draws a line between what you think is important and what he thinks is important. He sets up a conflict between your personal interests and your inculcated sense of duty just like Mama tries to do . . . and often (usually?) does.

Never mind that Mama falls back on histrionics, reminds you that your father worked seven jobs (at once!) to give you the good things in life, or that she used to walk through the snow (all year), uphill (both ways) to bring you a good, hot lunch every day when you were in school. It makes no difference if the Boss uses different words. Both appeal to what they hope and anticipate will be your guilty conscience. Why does this work?

The main reason is that the person who intentionally triggers this conflict within you knows what he is doing. He knows that he is setting normally *parallel value tracks* on a collision course. Because these conflicts are so common, we should spend a few moments examining them and why they are so effective.

Value tracks are the basis for many of our everyday operating assumptions, the expectations and actions we discussed earlier that allow us to live one day after the next without having to constantly go back and reestablish each and every relationship in our lives. Value tracks are the result of an internal calculus that informs us of the importance of different people and things in our lives. But it should not be supposed that we have one, overarching value track in our lives; rather, we have several. Hence the modifier parallel: for each set of different and separate circumstances in our lives, we have a set of values. But parallel value tracks are something we develop over time, as we mature and realize that different things can have equal, non-exclusive importance to us.

Every child has, at one point in time or another, asked another child "Are you my best friend?" This question poses a dilemma for the one asked because it requires a choice. But the child's mind, at the same time, is perfectly capable of saying "Yes, Janie is my best friend," or "Uncle Chris is my favorite uncle" or "Blue is my favorite color," each selection to the exclusion of all other possibilities. At the same time, however, the child's mind is also perfectly capable of making a different selection within a week, a day or even an hour. Asked again later, the same child is perfectly capable of saying that Katlin is her best friend, that Uncle Bill is her favorite uncle, or that red is now her favorite color. Children don't have or need parallel value tracks. One suffices, even if its values are continually shifting.

But as adults, we develop the knowledge that few things in life have to be exclusive. With the exception of the person who is our mate (a relationship that is supposed to be exclusive), we are free to have several favorites in other areas, several best friends, a wide variety of loyalties and affections. The child may ask, "Mommy, who's your favorite, me or my brother?" But the parent knows that both can be her favorite, that both can be loved equally. The parent knows that just as one has ten fingers to which one is equally attached, one can have several children to whom one is equally attached. And so it goes as we grow, particularly in the modern world in which we live. In childhood, old friends tend to be supplanted by new ones. The new best friend in seventh grade replaces the best friend with whom we went to third grade. As adults, however, we learn to treasure old friends, even as our lives change and we make new friends. We have a parallel value track that informs us that both sets of friends, old and new, are important.

Our lives, particularly in the modern, post-industrial world, are not integrated. Society has advanced to the point where our personal, private lives are almost totally separated from our working, professional lives. Living in one community and commuting to a job an hour away is just one common example of this dichotomy. Further, the expected separation of our outward performance from our inner needs/wants/desires/feelings—typified not only by the Boss's reaction to the problem of our flooded basement being a personal problem, but by the hundreds of social norms we observe every day—serves to further divide our everyday lives into a set of categories, as opposed to a whole or integrated experience. Thus, the average day may be divided into segments for home, family, work or community, and the segments rarely intersect:

- The Boss has already made it clear that he is extremely disinterested in our family problems . . . and he is, no doubt, equally disinterested in our activities as a Scout leader, a member of a congregation or as president of the local Elvis Fan Club.

- Our spouses may think we are wonderful husbands and wives and parents. But how much does he or she really know about our life at the office, the shop or the plant? More to the point, does he or she care?

- The guys at the Elks lodge or the Scout troop, the women at the Junior League or the Ladies Fire Auxiliary all think our contributions to the community are outstanding and just dandy. But how many of them know that we are overextended, can't pay our bills, have a dysfunctional sexual relationship with our husband or wife or are contemplating an affair?

In sum, what these few examples serve to illustrate is the fact that we generally segment not only the activities of our lives, but the parts of our lives that we share within each of these segments. We share only what is **safe**, only that which will not go beyond the expected social norms . . . only that which will not trespass beyond the accepted boundaries of each segment. And this is only for "normal" stuff. What do we do with information concerning the fact that we secretly gamble (and lose) hundreds of dollars a week, that we go home and quietly get smashed drunk every night before dinner, that we and our spouse are swingers or belong to a local nudist club? Do we actually tell people that we are, in fact, having an affair with a local minister or are being investigated for bankruptcy fraud by the local federal district attorney? What do we do with this information?

We hide it, of course!

We hide it; not only because (obviously) many of these things would be frowned upon by our extended circle of contacts, but also because they fit into none of the established segments that describe our everyday lives.

What all these examples should illustrate is the extent to which our lives are, in fact, segmented . . . divided into neat little pigeonholes we call home, family, work or community. And on a daily basis, we somehow juggle all these balls, being careful not to let much, if anything, from one segment slip into another. This alone should cause most people to need therapy! But beyond this is the question of how we accomplish this delicate, social balancing act.

We do it by having **parallel value tracks**, self-contained sets of norms that we apply to each and every situation under the operating assumption that they will not only guide us through the minefields of each respective situation, but will also cover all (or most) circumstances we will meet within each of these segments of our increasingly segmented lives.

Thus we have a value track for dealing with Mama, a value track for dealing with the Boss and our co-workers, a value track for dealing with our closest friends, one for dealing with more casual friends and acquaintances, another for dealing with our spouse, one for dealing with our kids, one for dealing with other people's kids and on and on and on. In each of these situations, our value track informs us of the importance of the person to us and how we are expected to act toward that person. The value track gives us an internal guide by which to measure the importance of that person's demands upon us, long-term and at the moment. It gives us a sense of what we can get away with, how much the other person can get away with, and how to proceed.

The important point to remember here is that parallel value tracks allow us to place roughly equal importance upon a wide range of disparate people and things. Thus the work value track says that the Boss and his desires are paramount. The family value track informs us that spouse and children are the most important. The bowling league value track tells us that we can't let our teammates down by not showing up for the big tournament. The community responsibility value track reminds us that it is important to volunteer and contribute our time to the Scouts, the church fundraiser and the park clean-up drive. Ordinarily, because our lives are so segmented, these parallel values, these separate value tracks, never come into conflict. But what about when they do?

When Mama calls and tells you that she was counting on you to bring her to the podiatrist (never mind that she never mentioned it before), the Mama value track kicks in and you weigh the fact that the request is coming from Mama, the fact that she has no other way to get to the good foot doctor, the fact that she's been limping for three months or the fact that the podiatrist was your idea to begin with. The Mama value track then weighs her request against whatever else you may have scheduled or planned for the time of her appointment. And, all other things being equal, you usually

EVERY ONE YOU HAVE TO BE IN A DAY...

agree to take Mama to see the amazing Dr. Bunion. You mentally agree to juggle your schedule, cancel lunch with the boys or girls, put off painting the shed until later, or whatever, because your Mama value track tells you that her request is important and you ought to honor it. Moreover, Mama counts on the fact that this calculus is going on in your head when she makes the request. In other words, her child value track, the set of assumptions that form the basis of her dealings with you, tells her that her request is within the norms of what will be accepted.

Similarly, the Boss knows that your Boss value track is busily informing you that your ass is on the line every time he makes a request. Further, he is counting on that calculation to win out over any and all other value tracks that are equally busy informing you of other obligations. Normally, you cave in and agree to the Boss' request precisely because the Boss value track is so busily informing you that your ass is on the line.

But what happens when Mama and the Boss make a request at the same time? Then you experience conflict. Why? It is not merely because two events conflict on the schedule. Rather, it is because your value tracks are in conflict. Pit Mama against the Boss and you have a conflict, not merely between events but also between values. Both are important to you, and you would like to satisfy both. But you can't. You simply cannot take Mama to the podiatrist and make the big presentation at the same time. So you have to make a choice, a decision, you would have rather been spared from making. You either have to tell Mama to cancel the appointment or tell the Boss to find someone else to impress Mr. Big.

When these things happen, we experience these mutually exclusive demands as conflict, as emotional pain or as negative emotions toward either Mama, the

Boss or both. Either way, what we are in fact experiencing is someone using neurotic conflict on us as a motivational tool. Plainly put, people who use neurotic conflict are trying to make us feel badly so we will do what they want . . . it's not nice, but it's **usually effective**.

<u>Competence</u>

A third way to motivate people is through a sense of competence, or to use the fancy buzzword from the late 1980s and early 1990s, **empowerment**. Whether we call it competence or empowerment, it essentially means that positive reinforcement is the basic tool for getting someone to do something. Think about that for a moment.

When you use aggression or neurotic conflict to motivate people, the fulcrum, the point of leverage employed, is a negative or detracting stimulus. It is either an actual or implied threat, or it is the deliberate establishment of a conflict between two or more of the other person's parallel value tracks. Beyond this, the byproduct or the consequence of that negative motivational stimulus is often competition, a very real (even if often subconscious) competition between the goals of the person being told what to do and the goals of the person doing the telling. This, in turn, sows the seeds of resentment and a lack of future cooperation. In other words, both aggression and neurotic conflict result in short-term gains, at best, because they all but guarantee conflict at some point in the future.

Why? There are several reasons.

In the long run, with the exception of those people who are fulfilling a private psychological need by letting someone else control them, most people both recognize and come to resent the repeated, imposed control of someone else. They resent the ego bruise associated with repeatedly being forced to cave in, eat crow, and submit. They also resent the parallel bruise that results from the conflict when their value tracks are artificially made to collide. To make this a bit more clear, perhaps we should take a moment to discuss the difference between *external* and *internal driving forces.*

ಈ ಈ ಈ

An **external driving force**, one imposed on us from the outside, generally causes us to act in a way we resent, whether this resentment is conscious or subliminal, articulated or repressed. The law says that we have to fork over the lion's share of our yearly income in taxes by April 15th. So, as April 15th approaches, we go nuts looking for the zillion tiny pieces of paper that pass for our financial records; we call our accountant and make nice-nice to make up for the fact that we haven't spoken to the guy in a year, and generally make ourselves crazy to meet the April 15th deadline. Why do we do this? For the common good? Is it because a resonant voice within us tells us that good citizens of the commonwealth pay their taxes on time for the common good?

No!

We do this because if we don't the IRS will come along and take everything anyway. Thus the driving force behind our compliance with the April 15th deadline is external, imposed on us from the outside.

Similarly, the person who, going through a divorce, is guilted into leaving 9/10 of his or her worldly belongings behind with the soon-to-be-ex-spouse is rarely acting out of either altruism or self-interest. Rather, the very fact that someone is pushing his or her guilt buttons ("Well, it's the least you can do since you're the one filing for the divorce.") illustrates that the driving force in the decision is, once again, external.

In these cases, we are not motivated; rather we are **coerced**, forced or manipulated into compliance.

Further, if we recognize that this negative motivation, or manipulation, breeds resentment, we must also realize that resentment, in turn, builds further resistance. In other words, the dictator who forces an office staff, a household (or a nation, for that matter) into submitting to his or her capricious will through the use of coercive motivation is sowing the seeds of his or her ultimate undoing because the acquiescence displayed by those being manipulated is not the product of loyalty.

The Boss, the spouse or Mama, therefore, who browbeats, guilts, threatens or in any other way manipulates others into doing his or her bidding, is building a potentially explosive reserve of resentment. In the short-term this will all but ensure that the next time the Boss, spouse or Mama wants something, the response will not be positive. Rather it will in all likelihood require yet more manipulation.

In the long-term, this behavior will result in the stored-up resentment being expressed as anything from disloyalty or petty vengeance to an explosion of built-up resentment.

But when confidence in a person's competence is used and expressed to motivate people, the byproduct is **cooperation**. Why? Because true motivation, in contrast to manipulation, comes from within, an **internal driving force**. True motivation says, "I want to do this, accomplish that, give of myself, my time and/or my talents." True motivation does not, therefore, engender resentment, because the ultimate driving force behind the person's actions comes from **within** his or her own concept of self-interest. The individual may be doing something for someone else, on behalf of someone or at the request of someone else. The difference is that the task, the request, the goal, has been accepted by the person as being not only not in conflict with self-interest, but as in agreement with self-interest and sense of self. The psychological term is called *altruistic egotism*, doing good for the sake of doing good because it comes back to you.

Competence as a motivating tool works because it speaks directly to the self-interest and/or sense of self of the person whose compliance, agreement, acquiescence or cooperation we seek. Later, using my soon-to-be-famous Cardless Card Trick, we will explore just how to accomplish the feat of getting someone else to accept our goals through consensus. For now, let's stay focused on the issue of competence.

Most of us have seen a parent yelling at his son when the boy strikes out or misses an easy fly ball, or at her daughter when young Jennifer stumbles or forgets her lines during an audition. In these cases, what does the insensitive parent usually say? Isn't it usually something along the lines of "How could you be so stupid/careless/clumsy/scatter-brained, etc.?" This is manipulation. It seeks to activate the child's fear of rejection, his self-doubt, and a host of other negative emotions to shame the child into not only deeply regretting the mistake he or she made on the ball field or the stage, but, further, to get the child to do better next time.

But we have also seen the parent who realized that the child did not want to fail, that the child wanted to do better. This parent reassures the child that he or she not only shares the goal, but also believes in the child's ability to achieve it. This parent takes the child aside, assures him or her that the mistake was just a mistake and that he or she can indeed do better next time. The same example holds true for the child who, failing a math test, is already frustrated before Mom or Dad gets into the picture. What would make more sense? Calling the child stupid or lazy, or encouraging him or her to try again?

It is all about trust and competence. Using competence as motivation, one would say to the child, "I believe you can, and as soon as you believe you can, you will." This is true empowerment, true motivation.

What form of motivation works most effectively for you? For most of us, recognition of our competence wins out. That makes sense, right? Don't we usually take on greater responsibility; agree to more effort, when we buy into the goal? Think about it: isn't this the essence of volunteerism? People go to great lengths in support of a goal in which they believe, even if they are not directly compensated for that effort. It stands to reason, therefore, that if we want something out of someone else, the best way to do it is to make our goal his or her goal as well. In a working environment, what would be the more likely motivator, being told that as low man on the totem pole you got stuck with a job no one else wanted, or being told that the task really is important and you were the best person to do it? Clearly, the second would get more people motivated to accomplish the task.

Finally, competence recognizes the intelligence and decision-making capacity of the person whose cooperation we want to engage. Explaining why a task, an assignment or a responsibility is important builds confidence and competence in a way a mere order, command or directive can never do. This holds true whether the person receiving the order is a child, an employee or a co-worker. And so, as we seek to understand the concept of **effective control**, we have to recognize four things:

1) Effective control, whether ours over someone else, or that of others over us, is the ability to get someone to do something he or she would not ordinarily do.

2) There are essentially three ways to apply effective control: aggression, neurotic conflict and competence.

3) Aggression and neurotic conflict are inherently negative in both their application and their result. Only competence results in a positive experience for both the one seeking cooperation and the one whose cooperation is being sought. Only competence plants the seeds for future cooperation as well.

4) We have a choice, therefore, in both the type of control mechanism to which we will respond and the type we will use on others.

Before we move completely away from the issue of control, there are two last aspects of this subject I want to discuss. The first is the question of who we allow to have control over us. The second issue is the question of things we control: what are their boundaries, how can we recognize them, and how should we respond to them?

So, let's go to Chapter 8 and take a long delayed look at those who have control over us, the authority figures in our lives.

CHAPTER 8

You Control the Vertical

≈ ≈ ≈

This is one of the **most important** chapters in the book because it will address the root of your make-up as a human being. We will examine **what you think** and exactly **why you think** the way you do. We will also discuss authority and just how much authority others should have over you. Specifically, we will discuss the concept of **authority figures** and how they impact and influence our lives from birth through adulthood.

What is an **authority figure**? Put simply, an authority figure is a person or set of persons we allow to have effective control over at least some portion of the actions that comprise our lives. This much is self-evident. But what we may fail to recognize is that authority figures also shape our personalities and self-images.

Let's begin with **one basic truth**: children are born naked not only physically, but mentally and emotionally as well. They are blank tablets upon which their behaviors—from the language(s) they speak to the foods they eat—their values, and views of relationships will be written before they are more than a few years old.

Most of what you know, most of what you do, and a great deal of who you are comes from these first formative years. Infants are born with three impulses: the impulse to satisfy hunger, the impulse to avoid pain or discomfort, and the impulse to respond to comfort and affection. The importance of the first we recognize: without sustenance, any living thing withers and dies. The second we recognize: an infant cries when he or she is wet, dirty, cold, hot, hungry or hurt. But equally important is that the child be sustained by comfort, love, and a sense of competence. Brian Tracy, author of *The Psychology of Achievement*, reminds us that, decades ago, several unfortunate experiments proved that children deprived of touch, comfort, and any sense of love also withered and died. In fact, their responses were not so different from children who had been deprived of food. Positive reinforcement, along with food and the relief of discomfort or pain, are essential to the survival of the young human animal.

The infant, we should stipulate, has no sense of self at this stage of life; infants are pure sensation. They are more akin to organisms than people. They do not recognize that any such person, as "I" exists. They have no sense of who "I" is. They do not like and they do not hate. Further, except for two hard-wired fears, a fear of falling and a fear of loud noises, they have no fears. They do not innately fear people or situations. And they certainly don't fear failure. All of these fears (and likes and dislikes) are, ultimately, **learned**. Children, in their "state of nature" are uninhibited, unafraid, and trusting. I don't think I have to tell you how much this changes over time.

Perhaps the first fear a child learns is the fear of losing the love of Mommy or Daddy or whomever the primary caregiver may be. Adults sense this and often use related measures to discipline their children. In essence, discipline is characterized by invoking responses to negative stimuli children are hard-wired to avoid. See if you recognize any of the following:

- Yelling loudly to disturb the child's comfort level.
- Spanking to trigger the child's avoidance of pain response.
- Tonal changes, changes in facial expressions or threatening actions voiced to show disapproval in order to trigger a fear of rejection in the child.

The parent, Mommy in most cases, thus becomes the child's first authority figure. The quid pro quo between child and authority figure is symbiotic in the sense that the child accepts that the authority figure has unquestioned **effective control** over his or her life in return for giving the authority figure unquestioned love, devotion, trust, and loyalty. The child effectively asks the authority figure for three things:

- ❖ Tell me who I am.
- ❖ Tell me what I'm worth.
- ❖ Tell me how to act.

The child's sense of self is not self-generated; rather, it comes from his or her parents or other primary caregiver. Positive messages result in a positive self-image; negative messages produce weak, poorly formed or negative self-images.

The recent experience of a close friend illustrates how important this can be, and how many children, while certainly told and taught how to act, are not really taught who they are or what they are worth. As those of you with sons in the Boy Scouts may be aware, the organization has instituted a new required merit badge called Family Life. To earn this particular badge, Scouts must complete several tasks, including projects undertaken with and for the benefit of the family. But there is also a requirement that the Scout make a list of the reasons he is important to his family.

My friend is a Scout leader and he recently had a number of boys working toward this merit badge. He was appalled, he told me, at how many of the boys had no idea whatsoever about why they were important to their respective families. The best answer most could come up with was a list of the chores they did around the house. To me, this clearly shows that these kids have already learned that their importance, their value, is determined by **what they do** and not by **who they are**.

But beyond self-image, the messages parents give to their children also generate a set of *operating attitudes* with which the child will eventually face the world. What is an Operating Attitude? Simply put, they are those senses of self-competence and ability with which we face the world. Just as an internal measuring stick tells us how wide a trench we can jump over, our operating attitudes act as a mental and emotional measuring stick assessing risk and the probabilities of success for us each time we face a challenging situation. Well armed by positive messages in early childhood, therefore, we face the world with a "**can-do**" attitude. Valid challenges are there to be met. We have confidence that we can undertake everything from relationships to a career. In other words, we know what we know.

This may appear self-evident, but it is actually somewhat more complicated. In reality, there are four stages of knowledge of competence. The first is **unconscious incompetence**, whereby we don't know what we don't know; we haven't even thought to ask the question at this stage. So, to ask a young child, "Do you know how to speak Italian?" is not a valid question because the child does not even know what Italian is. The child is unaware of the fact that he doesn't know how to speak Italian because the concept of speaking another language never occurred to him. However, once we've informed the child what Italian is and ask the question again, the child will answer, "No, I don't know how to speak Italian." The child has graduated to **conscious incompetence**, the awareness of knowledge he does not possess.

So, we teach the child Italian. The first time the child sets out to speak or listen to Italian unprompted, he has to listen carefully, to actively translate what he heard, form a reply, and think about the grammar and vocabulary to answer. This is **conscious competence**, or the stage of being aware of what we know in an active, "I'm using this knowledge right this minute" sort of way.

Finally, the child becomes fluent and does not have to translate either what he hears or what he wants to say; he simply understands and speaks Italian. This brings us full circle to **unconscious competence**, or the stage at which we no longer think about what we know. Why is this important?

Our operating attitudes fall into the category of unconscious knowledge. We have long since stopped actively thinking about what we are going to do, how we are going to reply to a situation or circumstance, and we simply do it. Thus, if positive messages throughout childhood have armed us with positive operating attitudes, then when the Boss tells us that he wants us to undertake a complicated assignment, our internal voice says, "**Can do!**"

I'LL SHOW YOU!

Can-Do Behaviors

Can-do behaviors are. . . .

- Clear-cut   Can-do translates into specific action.
- Constructive Can-do action enables you to improve performance.
- Current   Can-do is action that can be started immediately.
- Controllable Can-do is action over which you have direct control.

If these positive messages are lacking, however, the result is a weak, poorly formed or negative self-image. These, in turn, often produce a weak, poorly formed or negative sense of self-confidence. The "I have to but I can't" behavioral model we discussed earlier is very often the result of such a poor sense of self-competence. It is not actively thought about, but instead operates under the surface.

We have stated that children learn their basic behavioral, value, relationship and emotional patterns from their parents or other immediate caregivers. What this means is that negative habit patterns such as fear and punishment also come from the adults around the child. Destructive criticism is the root of many of these negative patterns. Let's examine a few.

The **inhibitive negative habit pattern**, the "I can't" part of the "I have to, but I can't" model, is essentially a fear of new experiences, new challenges. Remember, the first word/concept children learn is the word "No!" The second is "Don't!" Used to protect a child from danger, from breaking things, and from negative behavior, these are useful tools. However, when they become a **linguistic straight jacket**, used to keep a child quiet and/or docile, they sow the seeds of an inhibitive negative habit pattern later in life.

For example, let's consider the child of a nervous, overly protective mother. If the mother has an abnormal fear of water, she will more than likely transmit this fear to the child. Similarly, if her fear is of strange or new places, new people, food not cooked at home or a host of other possibilities, these too will be transmitted to the child. However, while each of these may have an individual impact—the child growing up sharing his or her parent's fear of water, strange or new places, new people or food not cooked at home—the overall impact of these continued, combined warnings will be to stunt the child's natural inquisitive impulses.

As an adolescent, teenager, and adult, this person will very likely be saddled with the "I can't" operating attitude, with each new challenge or situation fraught with self-doubt and an overarching desire to shrink from the challenge, to be relieved of the responsibility at hand, to be protected from the realities of life as he or she was as a child. This clearly ties in with the personality type we discussed earlier, the person who wants or even needs a continuing series of authority figures telling him or her what to do. In other words, this person never really outgrows the sense that "I can't" because I'm too young, too small, too frail, too weak, too incompetent.

The example of the post-Depression parent has been used to illustrate this set of attitudes. Many of those who grew up during the Great Depression never outgrew the sense of financial uncertainty. Twenty, thirty, even forty years later, many of these post-Depression adults still approach every purchasing decision with the operating attitude of "I can't afford it/I don't really need it/I'll do without it," regardless of what the actual financial circumstances may be. Thus, the person with an operating attitude that continually informs him that he can't, that everything from asking someone out on a date to taking a new job is too risky, continually tells himself that "I can't afford to try," resulting in a personal developmental paralysis.

Another manifestation of these negative messages in early childhood results from the aggression motivation model we also discussed above. In this model, the parent seeks to motivate the child by continually issuing a series of dictates, "You have to because I said so." Presented on issues from style of dress to choice of friends, recreation, and career path, the cumulative impact of this message is that not only is the child incompetent to make any choices by him or herself, but also that the only value the child has comes from being completely obedient, following the rules, and, effectively, never thinking for him or herself. How does this work? Why does it work?

We have stated that among the child's most basic, primal needs is the need to be loved. The fear of the loss of Mommy's or Daddy's love, continually reinforced by the manipulative parent, renders the child fearful that if he or she does not follow the rules, Mommy or Daddy will withhold love. Thus the child thinks, "I am only loved and only have value if I **follow the rules**." Further, he thinks, "I have no value in and of myself. My only value is by virtue of what I do, the degree to which, and the success with which, I follow the rules."

Oddly enough, this operating attitude can and often does result in the development of an "alpha" personality. But, you might ask, isn't the alpha personality the one who always takes charge? Yes and no.

Many alphas' dominance is both a mask and a symptom. It is, or can be, a mask to hide a deep-seated sense of inferiority. But more to the point, the competition it bespeaks is in actuality a life-long quest for approval. If the parent was the source of this need for rule-following approval, the alpha personality acts this way even with people and situations that have nothing to do with his parents. And this is the paradox. There is, in fact, a **merging of authority figures**.

The merging of authority figures is the end condition resulting from a process whereby the place, role, rights, and relationship with a person's primary authority figure are extended to all other actual or punitive authority figures in a person's life. Thus, the relationship with Mommy is automatically projected upon the good Sister Asthmatica, Pastor Peabody, Dr. Knowitall, Mr./Ms. Wonderful, the Boss and on and on and on. In other words, the way the person views Mommy (later known as Mama) is transferred to whichever authority figures claim effective control over the person in question, whether or not that figure actually has a right to that level of control (a subject we will examine in a few moments).

For a person with an "I can't/but I have to" operating attitude this means that almost anyone who takes it upon himself to tell this person what to do or what to think is almost automatically granted the status of a valid authority figure. And the advice, criticisms or commands are given the same unquestioned acceptance as were given to those of the primary authority figure in the person's life. This is a person who not only continues to accept the advice, criticisms or commands of Mama, but also finds himself browbeaten by his spouse or significant other, children, supervisors, co-workers, the Boss, and anyone else who chooses to tell him off. While the easy, colloquial analysis of this person's situation/personality is that he is simply a doormat, the actual process at work is a combination of an "I can't/but I have to" operating attitude combined with a merging of authority figures in his world view.

This person, in other words, accepts all criticisms as equally valid. And the result can often be a personal developmental paralysis that is exhibited by the person being constantly depressed, constantly wishing he had stood up to Mama, the Boss, spouse or significant other, the nosy neighbor and just about everyone else this milquetoast comes into contact with. This is the person who spends a small fortune on motivational tapes and take-charge-of-your-life books, attends self-actualization seminars at New Age camps in the Berkshires, and then follows it all up by caving in to the next self-styled authority figure he meets.

Why? Because for all the self-actualization he may attain, on his own, away from the seminars and the self-empowerment meetings, away from the solidarity rallies, the books, tapes and the slogans, alone in his bed with the covers pulled over his head, he really doesn't believe a word of it. Rather, he continues on in life forever listening to the little voice in his head telling him "I cant'/but I have to/but I can't/but I should/but I can't. . . ."

But what about the person who accepts no criticisms as valid? Is this person just full of him or herself? Is she just so insufferably self-possessed and confident that she will accept no authority from any source? Often the answer is "not really."

Rather, this person very often is exhibiting yet another twist in the standard "I can't/but I have to" model. Let's call it the **"I won't"** variation.

The "I can't/but I have to" person is unable to differentiate between her actual needs and wants and those of others, between her own actual capabilities and those demands or limitations imposed by an early-life authority figure. Extended to all (or most) later demands and/or limitations set by others due to a merging of authority figures, this person spends life buffeted by the never-ending demands and opinions of those around her, constantly trying to win their approval. In other words, this sort of person never really learned to say "**No!**" Her way of dealing with abnormal or over-the-line impositions from authority figures is to simply surrender, to acquiesce to win approval in the interest of peace, or because she lacks the will, strength or the confidence to fight back. In sum, she does not recognize, as humorist Garrison Keillor reminds us, "When people make you run, they have more power over you than if you stand, fight, and lose." And there's another side to this coin: the person who simply says, "I won't!"

Every pendulum has points of extreme at either ends of its arc. "I can't/but I have to" is one extreme, one end of this behavioral arc. It is the extreme of always saying, "yes," in voice or in action. But at the other end is the person who, similarly unable to draw a line between valid and invalid demands, between opinions offered by a valid voice and those that are intrusive, presumptuous and issue from no valid authority, responds by rejecting all demands, all other opinions, and all other voices.

Here again we see a merging of authority figures, but with the opposite result. For this person, "I won't" becomes the automatic response, the defense against demands, opinions, and/or intrusions against which he or she has developed no other resisting mechanism.

Very often exhibited in adolescence or the teenage years, this blanket defiance can often be traced to a dysfunctional relationship with the child's primary care-givers. If the parents, similar to those in our previous examples, utilize destructive criticism as a motivational tool, if they imbue the child with negative messages about his or her self-worth and value, if they are not the safe haven they ought to be, the message comes through that the child cannot or simply will not live up to their standards or expectations. Where one child may develop an almost compulsive quest for approval, constantly striving to be perfect to overcome this attitude, another child may simply turn off, rejecting both the relationship with and the authority of the authority figure. Thus, no matter what the rule, request or demand, the child simply says "**no!**" If this attitude is extended to authority figures beyond the parents, merged in the child's emotional sub-conscious with all subsequent authority figures, the child develops the "I won't" operating attitude.

This is the person sometimes sardonically referred to as having a "**problem with authority figures**." This person could become a discipline problem in school, in the Scouts, in the military or in almost any other setting. This person often develops into the lone wolf who fol-lows no fashion, follows no trends or reads no bestsellers, rejecting them simply because they are popular. This per-son is usually not a success in any hierarchical structure, is someone who, while he can work well with other mem-bers of a team, repeatedly clashes with the team leader, simply because he subconsciously rejects anyone's lead-ership. This is the person who deliberately does not attend the annual awards banquet or accept the Boss' invitation to a company picnic, the person who deliber-ately flouts the corporate dress code . . . the person who simply will not play by the rules everyone else accepts as part of the price of membership in a given family or professional circle. In essence, these not-quite-insignificant gestures are this person's way of saying, "**I won't and you can't make me.**"

This is the person who, while perhaps accomplished in other measures of professionalism, continually develops problems with a succession of supervisors. In each case, the supervisor detects a clear and unmistakable challenge to his or her authority issuing from this person. And what is that challenge?

It is the **operating attitude** that says, "Rather than try to meet your expectations and run the risk that I will fail, I refuse to even try. Rather than try to win your approval and perhaps fail, I will short circuit the potential ego bruise by rejecting the very concept that your approval has value."

Very often masked as independence, marching to one's own drummer or having an extraordinary sense of self, this behavior can be as dysfunctional as a slavish devotion to the approval of others. It can be dysfunctional if it gets in the way of success, happiness, and/or peace of mind. If the skirmishes this operating attitude continually anticipates and sets up lead to a never-ending series of frustrating results—everything from lost jobs and lost promotions to lost relationships—and thereby diminishes the person's overall happiness and contentment, then the operating attitude is dysfunctional.

We've discussed both extremes, both ends of the pendulum's arc. As you have probably realized, the midpoint in the arc represents the balance between always saying yes and always saying no. The midpoint represents the healthy, optimum response to the issue and existence of authority figures. What is this midpoint?

It is actually comprised of several facets:

- the recognition that the authority figures one meets later in life are not the same as the primary authority figures from early life;
- the recognition that not everyone claiming the status of authority figure actually has a right to that claim;
- the recognition that a valid authority figure in one setting or segment of our life is not necessarily a valid authority figure in (all) other segments of our lives; and
- the recognition that neither always saying yes nor always saying no is an appropriate response to the authority figures in our lives.

Without knowing your background, I cannot say whether you had a healthy, supportive childhood or upbringing. But let's say for argument's sake that your childhood environment was not as supportive as it might have been, or that your parents either sent you mixed signals or simply did not know how to give positive reinforcement. Further, let's say that, while you may not always say either yes or no, you very often find yourself conflicted by mutually exclusive demands upon your various value tracks, that you often feel put upon by others, that you find the Boss making demands on your personal time that you do not know how to refuse, that your mother-in-law makes you feel small and insignificant, that your brother-in-law makes you feel like a chump, that your children make you feel guilty, the pastor makes you feel like a hopeless sinner and in general you feel as though you were born under an unlucky star. What do you do?

Step one in all these situations is to choose to respond and not simply react. Remember, the person or situation that causes you to react is exercising more control over you than you are, and that's wrong. In reality, to the greatest extent possible, you should control the horizontal; you should control the vertical in your life. So **step one is choosing that control by not reacting**.

Responding, however, takes thought. It is not automatic. So **step two is thinking about putting things into perspective**. Thus, the accident blocking our way on the Interstate may move us to react by throwing a fit, but in reality it ought to be an occasion to 1) realize that it didn't happen just to make us late; 2) if we are late, perhaps we should have begun the trip earlier than we did; and 3) respond by using the time we're stuck for something else, from a pleasant daydream to drafting that memo we were planning on writing later anyway. But it also gives us a chance to put clashing value tracks into perspective. And that is **step three: separating our value tracks and our authority figures**.

Now, admittedly, if one of these clashing value tracks has to do with the Boss, this is not always easy. Because, as we noted earlier, with the Boss our job, paycheck, or promotion is usually on the line. But that does not mean that the authority the Boss does wield should be allowed to cross over into other areas of our lives. When we were children, Mommy was the complete and dominating authority figure. But the Boss is not Mommy, nor are we still children.

Much like rendering unto Caesar the things that are Caesar's, we can and should give the Boss his or her due deference. Giving him or her more than that, however, puts us at risk. Similarly, for various reasons, we want to keep peace with our intrusive mother-in-law, our pompous brother-in-law, the pastor, the neighbor, and the irksome guy who's the coach of our son's Little League team. For each we should and do have a value track, but that value track should be completely distinguished from the value track we had with Mommy as a child. In other words, when the Boss, the mother-in-law, the brother-in-law, the coach or the pastor goes beyond his or her rightful claims upon us, it is up to us to draw the line.

It is helpful to remember that not all figures in our lives that claim authority over us come with a rank or a title or announce their intention to dominate us. Many simply try to exert control by offering unwanted opinions, unneeded advice, unsolicited guidance, unwarranted criticisms, and unconscionable demands. Their claim to the mantle of authority figure, to the exercise of effective control over us, what we do, what we say, what we think and what we feel is implicit in the offering of the unwanted opinions, unneeded advice, unsolicited guidance, unwarranted criticisms, and unconscionable demands. But it is up to us to **either accept or reject** that claim.

We can choose to accept it, but that choice should reflect a conscious thought and not merely an "I have to" impulse. Similarly, we can choose to reject it. But here, too, the concept of choice should indicate that the rejection is more than just the "I won't" impulse kicking in.

But, let's say we do choose to reject the implicit claim on our lives being made by someone else. How do we do such a thing?

We could attempt to do it by reacting to the provocation of the moment, by blowing up and telling the person off, but if the person is the Boss, we may get fired. If the person is our mother-in-law or brother-in-law, the result may be an unnecessary family rupture. If the person is the coach, we could wind up hurting our son's interests. If the person is the pastor, we could find ourselves soon looking for another congregation. None of these outcomes is pleasant and all are exacerbated by the fact that by reacting we usually put ourselves in a bad light and lose in logic what we attempt to make up in volume, venom or biting sarcasm. However, by choosing to respond we come full circle and can pick the time, place, tone, and wording of our answer. By choosing to respond we give ourselves the opportunity to decide, rationally, whether this is really a fight worth fighting. By choosing to respond we claim for ourselves the freedom of action and decision others would deny us or take away from us with their demands, limitations, and intrusions. By **choosing to respond we can control the horizontal as well as the vertical**.

But there is more to this. Over the course of the last two chapters, we've discussed our frustration at things we can't control. We've also discussed the control other people seek to exert over us. This leaves one important part of the equation still to be covered: the things we can control. This is so important. Why?

The first reason echoes the prayer, "Lord, give me the strength to accept those things I cannot change, the courage to change those things I can, and the wisdom to know the difference." As human beings, the fact is that we spend an awful lot of mental, emotional, and even physical energy trying to exert control over things that are simply beyond our control, in other words, **trying to change things we can't change**. So this is one concept we should examine.

The second reason is that we often miss or fail to **take advantage of the opportunity to exert the control we do have**. In other words, we often lack the courage (or foresight, or will, or simple chutzpah) to change the things we can.

Finally, the confusion between these two is, in and

of itself, a common cause of frustration and pain, an ego bruising. The wisdom (or insight necessary) to know the difference is not there, or is not being allowed to operate. And this results in negative consequences for us and those around us.

I will begin by stating my essential premises.

There are only four things we control:

❖ What we do
❖ What we don't do
❖ How we act
❖ How we react or respond

What does this mean? To begin with, it means that there is an awful lot in life you don't control. Further, and this is very important, there are things we can't control.

The weather is one example. We can't control the weather and make it cooperate with our plans. So getting mad because your picnic, camping trip, family outing or even your entire vacation was ruined by rain is a waste of time and energy. "Well, I can't help it," you say. "It just pisses me off!" My answer is, "Oh, yes you can—if you choose to."

What does it mean to get angry, mad or pissed off? It means that, more often than not, you are reacting. To what? That is what needs to be examined. Let me explain.

Several sections ago, I introduced a chart illustrating the concept of FEAR or False Evidence/Emotion Appearing Real. Recall that FEAR and fear is not the same thing. True fear is a hard-wired response to a life-threatening situation or condition. So, if you come out of the restroom at work to find that the place is being held up by a bunch of crazed revolutionaries with machine guns, that tightening in your gut when they shoot a few bullets over your head is true fear. If there's an avalanche at the resort where you're skiing, a shark spotted off the beach where you're swimming, or a fire in the restaurant where you're eating, your gut tightens and your brain screams "Get me out of here!"

That's true fear and it's wired into your brain to keep your dopey self out of mortal physical danger; it's the fight or flight instinct we mentioned before.

Now, there are also times when your best guess tells you that there is danger ahead, even if you don't see the actual mechanism of that danger. For example, if you and I didn't know each other and I walked into the bank when you were doing your banking on a Thursday and I stuck my hand in my coat pocket and said to you, "Stick 'em up!" what would you do? Most likely, you would stick 'em up. After all, you have been conditioned by our environment and popular culture to think certain ways. That "stick 'em up" stuff is a stimulus you recognize, an activating event, as we said before, and it has a consequence, going back to good guys and bad guys, cops and robbers, cowboys and Indians. So, you react. And even though it's only my hand in my pocket and you cannot actually see the mechanism of the danger (the gun, which, by the way, I don't have!) your body responds to your brain's conditioned appraisal of potential danger, and you stick 'em up.

Here's another example. I'm from New York City and I've been conditioned, for good or ill, to think a certain way. If I'm going down the street and it's 11 o'clock at night and I hear a loud bang or a loud noise, my conditioned response is to either hit the dirt or to take off running as fast as I can. I'm not thinking that it may be a cat jumping up on a garbage can looking for food; I'm not thinking that maybe that cat knocked the top off the can. All I know is that I'm out of there.

What do we see in this example? We see an activating event, a stimulus. We see a conditioned interpretation of that event. We see a reaction. What we don't see, by my own knee-knocking, out-of-breath admission as I put as much distance as possible between me and the ax murderer, serial killer, biker gang (or cat) that made the loud noise I heard, was a **thought process**. Ah ha!

So, could it be that the difference between true fear and FEAR is that the former is not the product of a thinking process but the second is? As mentioned earlier, a common issue/problem is false emotion appearing real.

What does this mean? Simply put, it means seeing a bogeyman when there isn't one really there. The child who is afraid of the dark because "there are monsters there" is a prime example. We know that there are no monsters in the closet, under the bed or behind the bureau, but the child does not accept that fact. He or she believes that the monsters are there (you just can't see them at the moment) and is reacting to that emotion by exhibiting symptoms from hyperventilation to bed wetting. Of course, few adults still wet their beds. So what's the analogy?

Well, getting mad at an insult when no insult was intended is one example. Getting mad that fate put that accident in your way and prevented you from getting to the big meeting on time is another. But we've discussed this already. More to our point here is seeing the bogeyman in the form of a challenge when there isn't really a challenge there at all.

Here are some examples:

- I know he or she is irresponsible/selfish/frigid, but I'm going to change him or her.
- I know my mother is a nag, but if I fight her long enough she'll recognize the error of her ways and give me my space.
- I know life with a working spouse and 2.3 kids involved in ballet, softball, Scouts and the glee club is hectic, but, if I can get everyone in my household to work to the perfect schedule I've devised, I won't feel the pressure.
- I know I'm not the most important employee of Worldwide Amalgamated Yo-Yo, but if I can get my boss to focus upon the fact that I do my job exceptionally well and have all my paper clips consistently lined up with the fourth azimuth of the Sun, I will be not only spared from the pain of downsizing, but I'll get that promotion to the new plant in the south of France.
- I know he or she is not interested in me, doesn't take me seriously and is, in fact, attracted to someone else, but if I work at it hard enough, I can make him or her love me.

In essence, what we've listed here are impossible challenges. They represent a set of conditions we can't change, but we try anyhow. And what's the result when we face failure, time and again in these quests? More than likely, an ego bruise manifested as rejection, hurt, frustration, humiliation, anger or some other negative emotion.

What we see in these examples is a series of conditions, not unlike the weather, that must be accepted and dealt with, or rejected, on their own terms because in all probability, we are not going to change the irresponsible/selfish/frigid people in our life. Each is who he or she is. Our nagging, cajoling, pleading, yelling, screaming or crying is not going to change them. Oh, perhaps he or she will make some small display of change, but it probably will not last. And then what? We're back to nagging, cajoling, pleading, yelling, screaming or crying. And the cycle begins all over again.

The key is to recognize that the challenge we think we see, changing someone else for example, really is not there. Not only is it not a challenge, it is not even a logical choice. Oh, we can choose to take the situation as a challenge just as we can choose to believe that there really are bogeymen under the bed. But if the bogeymen are not really there in the first place, how can we be rid of them? Similarly, if the challenge was never there as a viable plan of action in the first place, how can we succeed?

Of course, there is one important difference between the weather and the examples we've listed above. That difference is the fact that while you may not be immediately able to remove yourself from the weather, you can remove yourself from many of these situations, or at least remove the situation from your life.

Remember, there are four things you unquestionably control:

- ❖ What you do
- ❖ What you don't do
- ❖ How you act
- ❖ How you react or respond

We do not and should not seek to control what others do or how they act. When we forget this, we are forgetting the third part of that old prayer, the part about the wisdom to know the difference between what we can change and what we cannot.

Recall our discussion of the concept of control. We

recognize how we resent it when others try to exert unwarranted control or influence over us. Doesn't it follow, then, that it would be wise to recognize the limitations of our influence over others?

Your father may have spent most of your life trying to dominate you, your actions, and your attitudes. You have fought him over this through the tender age of 43. But your father remains argumentative and opinionated. He also drinks too much, turning every family get-together into a screaming match by climbing onto his soapbox and telling off all within shouting distance. Can you change him? The answer is "**No!**" What are your options? Three come to mind:

1) You can accept his boorish actions and continue to attend these family gatherings for the larger good of the family and to enjoy the company of the rest of the clan, even though your father's actions will continue to upset you.

2) You can deal with his actions by refusing beforehand to allow him to draw you into one of his discussions and urging everyone else to simply turn him off and walk away when he starts ranting and raving. Thus isolated he will be deprived of what he needs most, an audience. Perhaps he'll leave. Perhaps he'll fall asleep. Perhaps he'll get bored and sulk. But you have dealt with it; you have exerted control by saying "I won't play any more."

3) You can refuse to attend any gathering where he also will be present. In making this decision, you will remove yourself from the situation. You will control what you are going to do and not do.

Are any of these choices easy? No. But neither is suffering the emotional tumult of being frustrated at the situation and your clear inability to get him to change his actions. It is indisputable, however, that focusing on what you control will, in the long run, feel better than focusing on what you can't.

CHAPTER 9

Beating You to the Ignore

ᨠ· ᨠ· ᨠ·

Those of you who remember the TV show M*A*S*H may recall a particular episode in which a new, young nurse joins the 4077th. Radar, the ultimate Peter Pan who, it seems, will never grow up, is immediately smitten with this young lady. But rather than trying to make her acquaintance, Radar pointedly avoids her after her first day in camp. When Hawkeye notices this apparently incongruous behavior, he asks Radar why he is avoiding the young lady to whom he's so obviously attracted. "Oh," Radar replies with forced nonchalance, "I'm beating her to the ignore."

The episode serves to illustrate something many of us do with much frequency, something we call *projection*. What is projection and how does it work?

Quite simply, projection is the process by which we project upon or ascribe to another person feelings and attitudes that actually originate within us. It is this process that tells the young man that not only will the young lady he is smitten with not take him seriously, but that she'll laugh at him and possibly ridicule him if he asks her out. Does the young man have any real basis for anticipating such a result? Perhaps. Maybe he is admittedly unattractive or unpopular. Perhaps she has a reputation for being beautiful, but cold and unfeeling. These things might be true, in which case he might be correct in rethinking his intention or desire to ask her out.

But he wants to ask her out; perhaps he even intends to do so. Getting in his way, however, is the surety he feels that she will reject his advances. In fact, he is so sure that she will reject him that he has even provided himself with the reasons she'll give, the manner and tone in which the rejection will be delivered, and (to his thinking) the probable social fallout that will follow. Mind you, the girl has not yet had the opportunity to actually say a word.

What is going on here? It may very well be that our young man has in fact already received subtle (or not so subtle) hints from her as to how she views him and, therefore, how she would probably respond to his invitation. It could also be that friends have made him aware of her feelings. In a case such as this, to which we will turn our attention in a few moments, the young man's conflict is actually between what he knows to be true and what he wishes was true. Sound familiar?

But if this is not the case, if the young man does not, in fact, have any hard evidence that he will be rejected, where does the belief that he will be rejected come from? The answer: from himself.

For the truth is that it is not the girl who is rejecting him; she has not yet had a chance to do so. Rather, his own poorly formed or negative self-image, his own insecurities are rejecting him. You'll recall that negative self-images, formed by negative value messages we receive during childhood, play an equally negative role in our everyday lives as adults. This is a facet of the "I can't" part of the "I have to/but I can't" model we discussed earlier. And it is the opposite of the "can do" operating attitude we talked about. Here, the young man is saying, "I have to (want to)/but I can't."

The mind is a sneaky thing. It will often tell us we can't do something, can't accomplish something, can't achieve, win, have, be worthy of or partake in something. But the mind doesn't particularly want us to know that it is issuing these messages that it is getting in our way. It needs a convenient scapegoat, someone or something else to blame, for stopping us. It needs an excuse for the lack of willpower, courage or self-belief that it is causing us to experience. So, the mind engages in projection.

While it is the mind of this young man that is telling him that he's not good enough for the young lady, it tells the conscious portion of the fellow's being that it is the young lady who feels this way. She then becomes the rejecting force; she becomes the villain, the cause of his pain. And she, quite possibly, becomes the object of his active or passive counterattack.

Let's return to Radar. His comment about beating the young nurse "**to the ignore**" is quite telling. In fact, Radar himself feels unworthy. He anticipates rejection (through projection) and counterattacks by treating the nurse rudely, by ignoring her before she has a chance to ignore him, by hurting her before she has the chance to hurt him.

Another example clarifies further. I have a patient, a woman of about 35 who has some issues with her mother. On many points, she is right. But on many, she is quite wrong. In one session we had together, she came in full of anger and quite upset over a recent incident during which she and her mother had had an argument. As we began, I asked her what was wrong. She launched into a tirade about her mother. For more than 15 minutes I never got a word in edgewise. Finally, stopping to take a breath, she asked what I thought. "Well," I said, "It seems that you're blaming your mother for an awful lot here."

That set her off. "Oh, sure," she said. "You're just like my sister and all the rest. You think I'm being unreasonable. You think I'm being selfish." She went on like this for several minutes. But the interesting thing is not what she said or what I said after this. It is the projection she engaged in that is of interest.

The truth is that she was the one who, somewhere deep down inside, agreed with her sister. She was the one who suspected that she was being unreasonable and selfish. Perhaps she was even the one who thought she was asking too much of her mother in the particular case at hand.

But for several reasons, she could not, would not admit this. The feelings had to come out in some way. And so a scapegoat was found; in this case it was me. I became the villain. I became the cause of her immediate pain, and I became the focus of her counterattack. Projection.

Projection occasionally works with positive feelings as well. Insufferable egotists will be absolutely sure their own perceived inestimable value is also perceived that way by the rest of the world. These people regularly assume we think as much of them as they do, that we'll be willing to grant whatever they ask simply because they are asking it and that we'll shoulder any burden, assume any responsibility and go to any length to make or keep them happy. Fortunately, these people are usually little more than a nuisance and, while they may annoy us, a counterattack by them rarely takes place because they're often too oblivious to realize that we don't necessarily want to do what they're asking, that we do not, in fact, think as much of them as they so obviously think of themselves.

But the person who engages in negative projection can be a problem because through this negative projection we are held accountable for thoughts and feelings we may not have. We are made to feel guilty for things we didn't think, do, say or intend; and we become the objects of a possible counterattack. What is a counterattack?

The counterattack is the last step in a process I call *thought reinforcement*. This process begins with a cause, a stimulus, and an event that gives rise to a thought. Let's say, for example, that the cause is a less-than-enthusiastic response on the part of our significant other to something we suggest. The thought that follows in this case may be "I'm unappreciated and unloved."

The effect of this thought is a feeling; in this case perhaps a feeling of deprivation and/or rejection. The result of this feeling is frustration. After all, there is discontinuity between what we want and/or expect and what we perceive.

And this frustration needs a release. This release takes place in two steps.

In **step one** we project upon our significant other the belief that we are unworthy of his or her love and that our efforts, whatever they may be, are not worth much and therefore hardly warrant appreciation. This explains to our conscious being why we think we are unloved and unappreciated. Interpreting this explanation as something unfair, we get angry. **Step two** is the actual release: we attack!

This attack can be either direct or indirect. A direct attack might involve saying something sarcastic, nasty or

otherwise cutting. The indirect attack, much like Radar's rude behavior to the young nurse, could be quietly efficient in its ability to hurt. Maybe we withdraw; maybe we sulk. Maybe we simply leave the house and let our significant other wonder what he or she did wrong this time.

Why do we do this? We may do it in the hope of affirmation, in the hope that our significant other will immediately see the error of his or her ways and come rushing over declaring undying love, devotion, and appreciation. But, we also do it in anticipation of the other's fighting back.

We know that our attack—whether direct, loud, and open or indirect, stealth-like and sneaky—will likely be interpreted as exactly what it is. And so, we prepare to defend ourselves from the reaction we anticipate. In Radar's case, he is rude to the nurse in the chow line: projection and attack. He then anticipates her response and gets ready for it. He sits in a corner by himself. Then, doing exactly what he expected her to do, she defends herself by sitting at yet another table and ignoring him. Wounded by her deference, he reacts by avoiding any place where he might even see her: counterattack!

In the process he has, through projection and attack, provoked her to fight back. When she does fight back, however, he proves to himself that his initial thought of being unworthy in her eyes was valid. He therefore reinforces his thinking.

I see you in a bar. I call over to you, but you're busy and don't really respond. I think you don't like me. This frustrates me. I seek release by a) telling myself that you're a stuffed shirt who thinks I'm a schmuck not worthy of your time, and b) saying something nasty about you within your hearing. You, upon hearing what I said, fight back by saying something cuttingly dismissive. I counterattack by saying something even nastier and walking out, now firm in my conviction that you're a stuffed shirt who thinks I'm a shmuck—which, by this point, you may.

Negative projection acts as a step in reinforced thinking by setting up artificial circumstances by which our darkest feelings, fears, and doubts are substantiated through the reactions we elicit in others. In truth, though, negative projection is an excuse, a cover for not facing and dispelling these feelings, fears, and doubts.

Let's return to my patient for a moment. Negative projection gave her the opportunity to get mad at me and avoid facing her own doubts about whether she was being fair with her mother. In the case of the young man wanting to ask the young lady out, negative projection gave him an excuse for not requesting a date, for not taking the chance. It also served as a convenient mask for his own insecurities and self-doubts.

When we engage in this negative projection, we are not only unnecessarily provoking a confrontation with the person upon whom we are projecting our own negative feelings, but we are also taking a step backwards. We are not facing either the challenge or the situation at hand, and we are not looking at our own self-doubts, the real cause of much of the negative feelings we project, in the full light of rational thought. In fact, by going through these motions, we are proving that our inner demons, our fears, self-doubts, and insecurities are controlling us to an extent we probably would not be comfortable admitting.

Which is better? Stumbling about letting these fears, self-doubts, and insecurities continue to get the best of us? Or facing them, tackling them, resolving and overcoming them? I am sure you see the obvious benefit of the second course of action.

Before we close this chapter and move on to an examination of you, I want to return briefly to those cases when sensing negative vibes is not projection at all, but, rather, is an early warning system telling us to get the heck out of wherever we are and whatever we're thinking of doing.

We've spoken of challenges and of our ability to accept and handle them. We have discussed positive operating attitudes and the difference between things we can control and things we can't. But there is another facet to all this: the issue of biting off more than we can chew.

For a moment, let's return to our young man and the date he desires with the young lady. All other things being equal, he probably should go for it. She may say "no," but she may say, "yes." But what about those little voices he keeps hearing in his head, the ones telling him he's nuts to even ask her?

Projection, perhaps? He could be projecting onto her all the fears, self-doubts, and insecurities he has about his own value and worth. But that little voice could also be his own sense of self-preservation screaming at him to cover his butt before it is too late.

Let's say our young man is short, portly, and generally dismissed as unattractive by most people. He is interested in little beyond UFOs and "The X-Files" and works as an assistant manager in the local doughnut shop when he is not hanging out at the neighborhood comic book store arguing the relative merits of the new Superman costume versus its traditional predecessor. She, on the other hand, is a vivacious former class president, the daughter of the town's leading banker, had her debut at the local country club, is regularly squired about by tanned young men in expensive cars, speaks three languages, and is attending an Ivy League college.

In this case, his infatuation with her aside, there are some good reasons for him to believe that she will indeed shoot him down if he asked her to go to a tractor pull with him. So, if he has second thoughts, it isn't projection; it may be common sense.

I offer this hyperbolic example to make a point: There are cases when it is prudence, not projection, that gives us pause or makes us think less of our chances than we might want to think. Answering a classified ad for a position as a Washington-based lobbyist when an individual has no experience in Washington is probably not going to result in an offer of a position. Thus, thinking, "I'm never going to get this job" as he puts his resume in the mail is not defeatist thinking or a projection of his self-doubts upon the firm doing the hiring. Rather, it is a realistic assessment of his chances.

This is important to recognize. Freud once said, "**Sometimes a cigar is just a cigar**." It is wise not to read too much into a situation. Sometimes you may be projecting; sometimes you may just be being prudent or sensitive to the very real vibes or signals someone else is giving. The important thing is to be aware of the possibility of projection and, when you catch yourself, to nip the impulse to project in the bud. As for when you're being prudent or sensitive to those very real, sometimes-negative vibes that everyone gives off, pat yourself on the back for your insight and move on.

We're about to turn to a subject that you will no doubt find fascinating: You. I'm going to ask some questions about what you think, why you think that way, and what went into making up the package you call you. I'll provide a set of questions, you'll provide the answers and together we'll try to figure out what it all means. It should be fun; it should be informative. And I can guarantee it will be interesting.

CHAPTER 10

Who . . . Who Are You?

·ā· ·ā· ·ā·

Now it's time to scratch the surface of the being, the entity, and the social animal called you.

First, let's review. We've discussed operating fantasies, assumptions, and presumptions. We've discussed value tracks; we've discussed conflicts, projection, and the "I have to/but I can't" paradigm. We've discussed "signposts up ahead," control, and relationships with others around us. But an element has been missing from this discussion. The missing element has been you.

Few of us truly know ourselves. Not only do we rarely see ourselves as others see us, but most of us get so caught up in the second-by-second living of our lives that the person we are becomes little more than a shell carrying around the self that we are.

Put differently; imagine you have something terribly important on your mind. That concern consumes you altogether. It is all you can think about. Meanwhile, there is the day to get through, during the course of which you encounter several other people. But because your self is preoccupied, your person, the entity everyone else sees and interacts with, appears to be on autopilot. You may come across as rude, distracted, spacey or any of a number of other things without intending to do so. This is true of the girl everyone thinks of as a flirt. In fact, she could be deeply insecure. Her self has tremendous doubts; her person is largely a mask. This is the separation between **person** and **self**.

So, when I ask, "Who are you?" you must separate your person and your self. Think of the person as being that part of you that is on the outside; the self is that part of you on the inside—the shell and the yolk, as it were.

Now, the outside, the person, is what everyone else sees, interacts with, likes or hates. Very often, too, the outside, the person, is our prime focus as well. It is our person who is concerned with whether there's a spot of spinach stuck between our teeth, whether our hair is combed perfectly, our breath fresh, our clothes fashionable, our car spiffy, our dance moves slick, our romantic/sex appeal effective. For instance, it is our person who goes on most first dates, while our self sits home like grandma with the porch light on, waiting to see how it all came out.

Here's a personal example. When I began graduate school, the first day of class was very sunny and very hot. I got dressed and headed out for my first class sometime around noon. I wore what I thought was appropriate: a pair of boots, recently polished, a pair of decent green pants cut in a style to imitate jeans, and an off-white, almost yellow shirt. Hey, what can I say? It was the '70s and I thought I looked pretty cool.

By the time I walked the mile and a half or so from my apartment to the campus, I was sweltering. So, as I entered the building, I unbuttoned my shirt a bit. Then, books under my arm, I sauntered into class and thought nothing more about it. As it happened, there was a woman in my class who I eventually came to know. We became friends after a while and one day she made the most amazing admission.

"You know," she said, "when I first saw you, I couldn't stand you."

I expressed my surprise. "Why?" I asked, incredulous.

"Because," she explained, "you looked so full of yourself, so arrogant."

"Full of myself? Arrogant? Me? Why?" I asked.

"Well," she explained, "first of all, there were those boots. . . ."

"But I *always* wear boots. . . ."

"And those pants. If they had been any tighter across your butt, they probably would have split. And then, of course, there was that shirt, unbuttoned down to your navel."

"It was *hot*," I sputtered.

"Well, you did swagger into the room like you owned the place, " she continued now obviously warming to her subject.

"*Me?* Swagger?"

It is probably a good thing that this woman and I were friends and never had any sort of romantic entanglement, because if we had I don't think we'd have ever gotten past that conversation. In time, I came to realize that what she reacted to that day was my person, specifically my made-in-New York person. She was from South Carolina. We had cultural differences. Eventually, she came to see, appreciate, and even like my self, hence her eventual statement that I was not at all like the person I came across as being that day.

The distinction between person and self is important for a number of reasons. One of the most basic reasons is the self and the person are largely separate and distinct in origin. In a nutshell, our person is largely, though not exclusively, self-created, while our self has roots that go back before conscious thought.

First, let's focus upon the person side of this equation.

When I ask who your person is, you might do best to ask other people, those around you every day. Why? Because there is an awful lot of person entwined in personality, and it is with our personality that most people around us interact. What would other people say about you?

They might say that you're funny, that you're thoughtful. They might say that you're self-centered, morose, a good sport or a bad loser. They might say that you're a goof-off or a good worker. They might say you're lazy, energetic, and emotionally distant or that you wear your heart on your sleeve. They might say that you're impossible to work with or that you're a hell of a guy.

Note that we've just listed 14 traits or adjectives. Some you may recognize in yourself and some you may not. But ask yourself this: Are any of these descriptions we've used words you would use to describe yourself (leaving out for now the glowing adjectives with which you've stuffed your resume)?

If you were on a first date and the other person said "So, tell me about yourself," would you begin with, "Well, I'm a hell of a guy"?

There are different things, all part of our make-up that others and we see about ourselves. Do you see yourself as trying to be funny, lazy or energetic? No, of course not. From your vantage point, you're just being you. So here we see the first facet of this dichotomy, the difference between the **inner self** and the **outward person**.

A second facet to be explored is the role of self-creation in our person.

Do you dance? Do you dance well? Well, if you do, there had to be a point in time when you decided that, for you, it was important to learn how to dance. You weren't born knowing how to dance, although being born with a sense of rhythm probably helps in this instance. The point is you learned to dance. If you ski, play the oboe, knit, build furniture, cook, bake, take on home improvement projects, wear all the latest fashions, if your make-up always looks professionally applied or if you're a whiz-bang computer programmer, you learned all of these things. There was a conscious decision somewhere in your past that prompted you to master these skills, to make them a part of the person everyone else sees.

Let's take fashion sense for a moment. There are people who dress very well. There are people who dress very poorly and there is the vast number of us somewhere in the middle. Now, if we disregard the obvious differences in income that allow some to wear the latest Paris fashions while others shop at Wal-Mart, we still see people we come into contact with every day who dress according to one of the three categories we just listed above. So, what distinguishes one group from the other?

One clear difference is that those who dress well want to do so and do something about it, whether that something is skimping on other expenses to afford the nicest clothes or simply taking the time to read the fashion magazines and constantly shop and renew their wardrobes. The point is that they are consciously doing something.

Those in the middle usually just want to look decent and that's as far as their effort takes them. Those who don't dress well, on the other hand, simply don't care.

What does this tell us? Well, for those who expend the effort and resources to look like fashion plates, image is a conscious part of their person. It is certainly something that stands out and something that others will notice. It is also clearly something on the outside and a self-constructed part of their overall outward person.

Similarly, the woman who becomes an ardent feminist or Christian and whose every comment or observation, it seems, is informed by that perspective learned the formal underpinnings of those views. Similarly, in crass counterpoint, the guy who tells the most racist jokes, who makes crude remarks about women and constantly talks about his (real or on-line) sexual contacts, learned those behaviors and adopted them for a reason. Maybe he thinks they make him seem like a big man, a "real" man or some other sort of superior being. Maybe he thinks that this sort of behavior will help him fit in better on the bowling league, on the assembly line or at the lunch counter. But, either way, he thinks he gets something out of this behavior. Maybe it is attention he is after. Maybe it is something else. But the point is that he is comfortable with these actions and attitudes and carries them out consciously for a reason. Again, his person, crude and distasteful as it may be, is a conscious construct.

So to return to the question of who you are, if we focus upon the person and use this new insight, we can probably come up with a list much like the one we outlined before: People might say that you're funny, that you're thoughtful. They might say that you're self-centered, morose, a good sport or a bad loser. They might say that you're a goof-off or a good worker. They might say you're lazy, energetic, and emotionally distant or that you wear your heart on your sleeve. They might say that you're impossible to work with or that you're a hell of a guy.

But what about your **self**? What is that? Where does it come from and what informs its internal logic?

A clue can be found in the very common contradictions that we observe between the person and the self in those close to us. We see the man or woman whose person is confident, flirtatious or even bombastic, but who is riddled with self–doubt and insecurities and is given to depression and self-deprecating outbursts. We see the person who views his self as kind and giving while everyone else around him sees his person as prickly, spoiled, irrational, and volatile. We see the woman whose person everyone sees as virtuous, giving, honest, demure, and perhaps even a bit prudish, while she sees her self as of low moral character, perhaps a failure as a mother or wife.

From where do these contradictions originate?

As we have established, the person is largely, if not exclusively, a conscious construct. In many ways, we consciously decide how we want others to view us and take steps to create that look, style, attitude or manner. Our person can, and often does, change over time with experience, maturity, and an altered perspective. Hence, the philandering lad who repeatedly embarrasses himself and his wife may become, with time, the doting husband and father. The petty thief can go straight, and the substance abuser can turn his life around. The shiftless young man can become the industrious provider, and the carefree party girl can become the staunch mate and mother. The person can and does change and very often it is as the result of a conscious decision. But what about the self?

We have already spoken about the influence parents and primary caregivers have on the emotional development of a child. We have discussed how negative messages can and do result in poorly formed self-images, a lack of confidence, and other emotional or behavioral shackles. But let's take this a step further.

At the outset of this section we asked, "Who are you?" We have established that there is a difference between the person the outside world sees and the self almost no one sees. We have also established that whatever your person may be, you've had a large hand in creating that outside image, probably since you were in your teens. But what about your self? Where did that come from?

If we accept that many of the characteristics of self (the anxiety and insecurities or the "can do" attitude we have, the "I have to/but I can't/but I must/but I don't want to" model we struggle with, or the empowered sense of competence that helps us meet and overcome obstacles) come from our earliest experiences, then we must turn there for an answer to the question of "Who are you?"

There are two primary sources of self. The first is wrapped deep somewhere within your DNA. That genetic code determined whether you'd be smart or dull, good with your hands, good with languages, good with mechanical models or abstract concepts. It determined whether you'd have a flair for art or a talent for music. It determined whether you'd like spicy foods or whether a more bland flavor would be more to your liking. In part, it may even have determined your attitudes toward sex and sexuality, your attraction toward one sex, the other or both, and whether you are comfortable with physical expressions of affection.

But, in a sense, all this genetic code was the raw material of your self. It would be as though a clay maker had the ability to produce several different types of clay. Some might be more malleable than others; some might take to pigments better than others. Some might harden quickly, and some require baking to really dry and harden. Yet, when all is said and done, the stuff is still clay. It is a lump, formless, and largely without function, its characteristics laying fallow and unused.

Enter the potter. He or she may be skilled or quite unskilled. He or she might have a flair for the dramatic in design and form or tend toward the spare and utilitarian. He or she might select a particular clay for its properties or just use whatever is at hand, never exploiting the special properties that even the materials at hand might have. Either way, it is the potter who gives form and shape to the clay.

So it is with us. Our DNA gave the clay of our basic selves its properties, its characteristics, its strength or malleability. But our earliest experiences; the influences of parents and other primary caregivers; our relationships with siblings, friends and our families' immediate social circle; our families' place in the neighborhood, the parish or the congregation all contributed as the other source of our self. Just as the potter gives form to the clay, these influences helped give form to our self.

And just as the potter has no control over how the object he or she has created from the raw clay will ultimately be used by the consumer who buys it, those who influenced us early in life, who helped shape our self, have little ultimate influence over the use to which we put that self, the person that self leads us to create. The father can do all within his power to teach his son right from wrong, a sense of responsibility, and the value of a good work ethic, only to see the son wind up in jail. The mother can do all she can and still see her daughter lost to drugs or making porno films.

Similarly, a parent can be a terrible influence and yet have offspring who thrive, succeed and grow way beyond the limitations imposed by that parent's actions and/or attitudes.

In the end, we are much like the consumer who buys the object the potter has made: We had absolutely no influence over the make-up of the clay and little if any influence over the form that clay took in the potter's hands. But once it is ours, **the responsibility for what we do with it is ours**. So, too, we obviously had no control over our genetic make-up. Our influence, in turn, over the influence our parents, family, and social setting had upon us was likewise minimal if it existed at all. But when we come into our own, when we begin to construct our person, it is up to us to make the most of what we were given.

WHAT SHAPE ARE YOU IN?

CHAPTER 11

If I Was a Rich Man

ࢠ ࢠ ࢠ

If I was a rich man, truly rich, I'd probably be a lot of things—and one of them is that I probably wouldn't be my father's son. But I was and I am and those experiences, the influences of the home in which I was born, gave me, together with the DNA wrapped deep somewhere down in every cell of my body, the stuff of my self.

It's the same for you.

Now, I know who I am and how the influences and environment of my early years helped make me the wonderful, caring, compassionate, intelligent, sexy, suave, hell-of-a-guy I am today.

But what about you?

Very early in this book, I wrote that it was going to be, at least in part, an interactive process. In the following pages, I am going to present you with a survey of sorts. I'd like you to take some time to answer the questions. Go ahead and again write in the book.

Take your time to answer all the questions as best you can. Some of them require simple, one-word answers. Others you may have to think about. Either way, I'll be there when you finish, just a few pages away.

❧ ❧ ❧

Background Questionnaire:

Last name: _____ *Gable* _____

What is your age? ____ *42* _____

What is your ethnic Origin? *American* _____

Where are you from? ____ *Albany* _____

Did you grow up in an urban, suburban or rural setting?
_____

Was it a wealthy, middle-class, working-class or poor
community? _____

Was it a close-knit or fairly anonymous community?
_____

Looking back, would you say it was a liberal or conservative community in its values, though not necessarily
in its politics? _____

Were both your parents alive when you grew up?
_____

If so, what was the relationship between your parents
like, as husband and wife? *Love & hate* _____
_____

_____

*(If your parents were divorced, widowed and/or remarried,
modify the question and answer about your mom and step-dad
or dad and step-mom.)*

What were your parents' (step-parents) attitudes toward public displays of affection? _Very_ ✓

_____

_____

What were your parents' (step-parents') modes of communication? Were they open? Did they truly communicate? Did they argue in front of you? To what degree, how often and about what? _____

_____ ? not much memory of _____
_____ any _____

_____ left → college 17 _____

_____

_____

_____

_____

Did your parents make up quickly after a fight or argument? _yes_

What was your father's occupation; was it white collar or blue collar? _w_

What sort of hours did your father work? _8-5_

How many days a week did your father work? _4_

What was your mother's occupation? _R.N_

What sort of hours did your mother work? _X x^4_____

_____

How many days a week did your mother work? _____

_____ 3-4 _____

What did you learn about the way men treat women
from the way your father treated your mother or step-
mother? _____

_____ MOM → WORKHORSE _____

_____ DAD → more $ _____

_____

_____

_____

_____

_____

_____

What was your relationship with your father? What
was the balance between the praise or criticism you
received from him? _____

_____ Dad → not much praise _____

_____ did not value _____

_____ women as = _____

_____ wanted me to be hyg.- _____

_____

_____ 1200 SATS at 16 y. or
mom said no way!

What did you learn about the way women treat men from the way your mother treated your father or step-father?

waited on him —
however my mom was
smarter then my dad — academically
my mom went to college at 16
B.S. —

Dad had $ → never worked hard
but a smart

What was your relationship with your mother? What was the balance between the praise or criticism you received from her?

Mom my best friend
however very tough on me.
academically / psyhical —

Did you have any siblings? 1

How many?

How many older than you, how many younger?

J.J.G

What was your relationship with them? _____

_____

_____

_____

_____

_____

_____

_____

_____

What are those relationships like today? _____

_____

_____

_____

_____

_____

_____

_____

What were their relationships with each other like? ___

_____

_____

_____

_____

_____

_____

_____

_____

What are those relationships like today? _____

_____

_____

_____

_____

_____

_____

_____

_____

_____

Were academics stressed as a family value while you
were growing up? *Yes most placed on*
my self - dad didn't expect M

Was it more than simply behaving in school? *Yes*

_____

What was your family's religion? *R C.*

Was religion stressed as a family value or was the accent
simply on attending services? *Yes*

_____

Did your family vacation together? *Yes*

Did you participate in activities as a family? *Yes*

What sort? *Skiing*
Vacation
track

Did the family eat at least one meal a day together?

_____

If you are a woman, how, when and from whom did
you learn about menstruation? _____

_____

_____

_____

_____

_____

_____

_____

_____

How, when and from whom did you learn about sex?

_____

_____

_____

_____

_____

_____

_____

Beyond the mechanics of reproduction, how, when and
from whom did you learn about sexuality? _____

_____

_____

_____

_____

_____

What were the messages or impressions, if any, you received from your parents regarding sex and sexuality?

Don't have sex when you're married

Did your parents engage in or participate in any community organizations or activities?

? probably

As a child, did you or did your siblings participate in community activities? (Boy /Girl Scouts, 4-H, CYO, JCC, Little League, Pop Warner, Classy Lassies, etc.)?

What do you remember about your junior high school years? What is your impression of that time in your life? _____

_____

_____

_____

_____

_____

_____

_____

_____

What do you remember about your high school years? What is your impression of that time in your life? _____

_____

_____

_____

_____

_____

_____

_____

_____

Did you have any significant romantic relationships during your high school years? _____

_____

How many? _____

Were they healthy relationships? _____

What about a work ethic? When did you take your first part-time job? _15_

What was it? _Bill Drafting – Budget_

Were your parents in favor or against the idea of you working? _got me job – approved $_

Did you participate in sports in high school? _Yes_

Did you participate in other school activities? _Yes_

Would you say you were popular in high school? _middle_

With the boys? _Yes_

With the girls? _rude_

When did you graduate from high school or receive a GED? _____

Was it assumed by your family that you would go to college after high school? _yes_

Did you go to college? If so, list all that you attended.

_____
_____
_____
_____
_____

If you didn't go to college, what did you do after high school? _____

_____
_____
_____
_____

If you did go to college, what was your major? _____

_____
_____

What were the most significant experiences you had during those years (besides partying)? _____

_____
_____
_____
_____
_____
_____

Did you have any significant romantic relationships during these years? _____

How many? _____

_____

Were they healthy relationships? _____

_____

Did you participate in any school activities in college?

Young Republicans

intercollegiate

_8m_

What would you say were your major accomplishments
during these years?

A's GPA

great Bf

ża ża ża

**Now, a bit about you since those days, right up to
today:**

What are your living arrangements today? (Are you
married, divorced, single, re-married, a widow or wid-
ower, living with someone)?

Do you have any children or stepchildren? _____

_____

_____

Are they living with you? _____

_____

_____

Did you continue your education? _____

_____

_____

What has your work history been? _____

_____

_____

_____

_____

_____

_____

_____

_____

_____

_____

_____

_____

_____

        Now that you have answered these questions, we
need to take a look at the evolutionary not revolutionary
conditions of your past that have conditioned you to
think in certain ways about yourself. Examples might
include your having low self-esteem issues from childhood because you received more negative criticism than
positive praise. Your parents might have split or divorced
at an early age and you have abandonment issues today

or don't trust the opposite sex because one of your parents had an affair. Coming from an addictive family environment, where alcohol, drugs (prescription or otherwise), gambling, excessive eating, etc. were present, may have caused you to be an addictive personality or type A personality today. Growing up as an only child may have resulted in you having issues with differentiating between being self-centered and selfish. Finally, you may have grown up in a normal family environment, but past choices may still be consciously or unconsciously causing you guilt feelings. The key is to look for patterns from your developmental years.

Remember the formula: "What we are taught we practice, and what we practice we become."

What patterns do you begin to see? _____

_____

_____

_____

_____

_____

_____

_____

_____

❦ ❦ ❦

I BELIEVE THEY CALL THIS "EXCESS BAGGAGE."

CHAPTER 12

50 Ways to Leave Your Lover

ᴥ ᴥ ᴥ

If Paul Simon is right and there are fifty ways to leave your lover, then there must be at least that many ways to make other significant changes in your life—though not all of them will be the right, or best, ways to approach the problem. Dynamite, for example, might get rid of the squirrels that have taken up residence in your attic, but you may lose the attic in the process. So the key is to find appropriate ways to address a given problem without creating even larger problems in its wake.

Take, for example, problems with co-workers or supervisors; quitting your job can solve these. But the solution may not feel like much of a solution once you're standing on the unemployment line, and the mortgage payment is due. Similarly, demanding a divorce in response to the messiness of your mate is going a bit overboard.

Let's approach this systematically. Interestingly, it is possible to categorize your options. You can:

- Give up and learn to live with things as they are;
- Blame the rest of the world for your woes;
- Stick to the way you've been doing things in the hope that the world will change; or
- Change the way you've been doing things.

Now, the first option means you'll have to suffer in silence for the rest of your days. So, if that's your choice, consider yourself nominated for sainthood and know we expect no more complaints from you. The second option won't improve anything and will probably garner you no more sympathy than you're already getting. The third option brings to mind a comment by Bill Cosby to the effect that the best part about banging your head against a wall is that it feels so good when you stop.

That leaves only the fourth option, which is the subject of this chapter, **changing your thoughts that will change your behavior**.

What we need to think about is a *well-formed outcome*, the attainment of a worthwhile goal, and certain rewards. But this well-formed outcome must fit within certain parameters. It has to be realistic, something we can reasonably attain.

So, telling you I want to run for President of the United States is probably not realistic. I don't have the family name of George W. Bush, the name recognition of John Glenn, the political stature of Bill Bradley or the money of Steve Forbes to buy my way into the game. This being the case, a well-formed outcome is hardly likely to be the result, the wrestler Governor of Minnesota notwithstanding.

If I told you I planned to win the lottery, your response would be the same. The lottery is pure chance so nothing I do, beyond buying more lottery tickets, will improve my chances. I have no control and no potential for control over the outcome so, by definition, it cannot be what we refer to here as well-formed.

But there are outcomes which are both realistic and over which we do have some degree of control. A new job in our field or an improved relationship with our boss, parents, children or significant other are both worthy goals, as well as being realistic and something over which we have a degree of control.

Now, just as there is nothing certain in this life except death and taxes, there is no certainty we will achieve set goals. There are other variables, not the least of which include the personalities of others. So I hope I won't get mail from my readers saying, "Mark, I tried to facilitate my environment and improve my relationship with my mother-in-law, but it didn't work. She's still an idiot and she's still in my face!"

Here's an example I (modestly) call Dr. Mark's Incredible-Yet-Not-So-Famous Cardless Card Trick. In my hand is a piece of paper. On the paper is written the name of a card from an ordinary playing deck. Now, in a deck of cards, there are two colors: black and red. Agree? [You say, "yes" here.] OK, pick a color and tell me which color you choose. Ah, you picked black, so that leaves us with red. In red, there are two suits; there are hearts and there are diamonds. Agree? [You say, "yes" here.] OK, pick one suit and tell me what it is. Hmmm, I see you've picked diamonds. Okay. Now, in diamonds, there are picture cards and there are number cards. Would you agree? [You say, "yes" here yet again.] Between pictures and numbers, pick one. So, you've picked numbers. So that leaves us with pictures. In pictures there are pairs. There's the Jack and the Queen and there's the King and the Ace. Agree? Good. Pick one and tell me what it is. Interesting, you've picked the King and the Ace. All right.

Now, between the King and the Ace, pick one. Whoa! You picked the Ace. OK, so that leaves us with the King. Now, take a look at the piece of paper and tell me what it says.

You're amazed! It says King of Diamonds. And what card did I just say we were left with? Ah, ha! The King of Diamonds.

How did I do it? Well, I had a well-formed idea about what the outcome would be. I had already written down the King of Diamonds, right? Well, this card trick illustrates the nature of goal setting or planning. I knew where I wanted to end up, at the King of Diamonds. So I worked to facilitate my environment.

How? Well, after I said that there are two colors in a deck of cards, I then asked if you agreed. So, the first thing we learn is that we came to **consensus**. I then asked you to pick between black and red, the two colors in the deck of cards. You picked black, but black was not in my best interest. Remember, I want the King of diamonds— a red card. So, I began by establishing that, even though you picked black and my well-formed outcome was a red card, we nonetheless had an initial consensus on the terms of the exercise; we agreed that there were two colors.

You agreed with me that there were two color possibilities, black and red. But you picked black, an initial outcome that was not in my best interest. So my goal became to facilitate my environment.

There is a process called *default decision-making*. I got you to agree that picking black left us with red. In other words, I discarded your selection, black, and shifted the focus of the discussion over to red. I said, "In red there are hearts and diamonds." The conversation continued with red as the point of our combined attention and, from that point on, we were already working on my turf.

When I said, "In red there are hearts and there are diamonds. Would you agree?" I was working toward consensus for a second time, getting you to agree with the inarguable, so I could prompt you to agree to what I wanted.

I asked you to pick between hearts and diamonds. You picked diamonds and I didn't say a thing; I just crossed out the heart. The lesson here is that I used **silence** as a way to facilitate my environment. Next I said, "In diamonds there are picture cards and there are number cards. Would you agree?" You could not argue with that, so we established consensus again, for the third time.

I said, "Choose pictures or numbers." You picked numbers. But again, you did not respond in a way that suited my best interest; so I crossed out numbers again, using the process called default decision-making. I now had you focused on picture cards.

I said, "In pictures, there are two pairs: the Jack and the Queen, and the King and Ace. Would you agree?" Again, you conceded, saying yes, this being the fourth time we came to consensus. Asking you to pick one, you selected the King and Ace, so I crossed out the Jack and the Queen and didn't say a thing (again using silence).

"Now," I said, "choose between the Ace and King." You picked the Ace—definitely not in my self-interest. So, again, using the method of default decision-making, I crossed out the selection you made and that, my friend, left us right where I wanted to be. In spite of yourself, we ended up with the King of Diamonds.

CARDLESS CARD TRICK

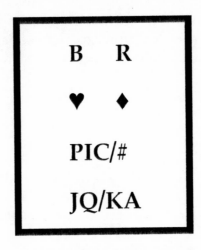

- **Know your well-formed outcome**
- **Facilitate your environment**
  - ✔ **Come to consensus**
  - ✔ **Use default decision-making**
  - ✔ **Use silence**

S.T.F.

STOP—THINK—FACILITATE

This illustrates a point. To know where you want to end up, you must define what your well-formed outcome is. What is your objective? What is your goal? What do you want the end product to be? My outcome—in this case the King of diamonds—was identified and established before we began the exercise.

The other consideration is how to facilitate your environment in order to get what you want. The answer, as our card trick shows, is to arrange things in a fashion that facilitates your achieving your well-formed outcome.

If you want to improve your relationship with the boss, your kids, significant other or your mother-in-law, you must first think about the goal, consider it, and ponder it. Make sure that it is reasonable, attainable and is what you really want. Then, having identified the goal, formulate a plan to achieve your well-formed outcome. To put it simply: **Stop, Think and Facilitate**. Use these three watchwords as we chart our course.

If changing your life were really just that simple, life would be easy, therapists would have far fewer patients, and this book would be a lot shorter. But the unfortunate truth is that, while we noted earlier that most people can think, we should also probably take note of the fact that few people do, especially in tense, emotional or frustrating situations.

As we looked at the background questionnaire in Chapter 11 and learned how we have been conditioned to think, here in Chapter 12 I am asking you to cut the past loose. There is no future in living in the past. So first we learn what our past has been, (the educational phase) and now in the rehearsal phase, I ask you to define what you want and determine whether it is realistic. Freud called this the pleasure/pain principle, and as you might know, not everyone chooses pleasure over pain.

So, before we move on to creating a new-and-improved you, lets take a look at some of the things that might be standing in the way of achieving the well-formed outcomes you'd like and deserve.

We've just discussed the Cardless Card Trick, a means of illustrating how you can facilitate your environment to get to your well-formed outcome. Now, let's discuss another methodology that we often employ that is not nearly as effective. I call it **Clueless**.

If the Cardless Card Trick was designed to illustrate at least one way to facilitate your environment, Clueless is an equally nifty illustration of how to fail. In fact, by following this method, you will learn how to amaze your friends, compound your previous mistakes, and make a complete disaster of your life. And the best part is, it's easy. All you have to do is completely ignore the three watchwords we mentioned a page ago. In other words, **don't stop**, **don't think**, and **don't facilitate**.

How do you do that? Easy. **Just act before you think**.

Let me offer some examples. Some time ago I was due at an important meeting. Preparations for it were consuming all my thinking. In the middle of the meeting, I was informed I had a phone call. Somewhat embarrassed, and more than a little annoyed, I took the call. It was my wife.

It turns out that in my haste and single-mindedness to get ready for the meeting, I'd left the house unlocked and several things out of place. When my wife came home she immediately suspected that the house had been broken into and reacted accordingly: She was afraid and a little angry too. Once she'd discovered we'd not been robbed, however, she wondered if I might have been responsible for the condition in which she found the house. So she called.

Now, I've got to be honest. An unlocked back door was not the foremost thing on my mind right then. I was focused on the meeting. As soon as I got on the phone, she began screaming at me. My well-formed outcome for the day was the successful completion of the meeting.

The phone call from my wife was an unanticipated bump in the road. The question was how could I continue to pursue my well-formed outcome in the face of her angry phone call? Clearly, I had to defuse the situation with her before I could return my attention to the meeting.

Now, when someone is yelling at me my instinctive reaction (Cute, huh? I said reaction not response; we've heard this before) is to yell back. So there I was, having just stepped out of a meeting, and my wife was screaming at me. What did I want to do? I wanted to yell louder, call her two names, and be at least three times nastier than she was being. After all, isn't that the way to win an argument? Ah, my past-conditioned thinking or embedded belief system told me: "He or she who yells loudest wins." Talk about being clueless!

But, notice that I said that my instinctive reaction in these situations is to yell. By definition then, yelling would not be a thinking response. Remember: stop, think and facilitate. Yelling right back into the phone, making my blood pressure sky rocket while completely losing my composure and my train of thought would not, in all likelihood, help me continue the pursuit of my well-formed outcome. In other words, yelling does not stop yelling.

How many times have you been in a store or some other public place and seen a child acting up and crying? How many times in this situation have you seen the child's parent lose his or her temper, whack the kid's bottom and say, "Stop crying before I really give you something to cry about!" Now, has it ever dawned on you as it has on me that inflicting pain (whacking the child's bottom) is itself a cause for a child to cry and is not the way to get a child to stop crying? Well, then, if hitting a crying child is not going to make him or her stop crying, why then should yelling back at a yelling person make him or her stop yelling? Wouldn't common sense suggest that there just might be a better way to address the situation?

Well, yes. But remember, if we employ the rules of being Clueless, then we must yell, stomp, scream, threaten, bluster, bawl, screech, shriek, and generally act like an idiot in the face of someone who is loudly and perhaps abusively angry with us. In other words, don't stop, don't think, and by all means don't facilitate.

Recognizing that there are two sides to every coin, or to every story, is perhaps one of the best tools at your disposal if you are trying to achieve a well-formed outcome. In other words, the choice is yours: The Cardless Card Trick or its Clueless counterpart. Which makes more sense?

Of course, there's always the little matter that it feels good to blow off some steam once in a while. But as Star Trek's Mr. Spock would observe, it is also **illogical**. If our goal in any situation is our well-formed outcome, pushing back in an emotionally charged situation will not gain the cooperation we seek. It's more likely to make the other person, boss or spouse, dig in deeper. The crying child rarely stops crying when he or she is hit, so why should an angry or frustrated adult become any less so if we respond with anger or frustration of our own?

The Cardless Card Trick illustrates several ways to get where you want to go. If I'd thrown all the cards in the air and declared you an idiot the first time you'd selected a card I didn't want you to select, where would we be? Or more importantly, where would I be? I certainly wouldn't have been able to facilitate my environment of you choosing the King of diamonds, would I?

❦ ❦ ❦

Chapter 13

Tell Me What You Really Want

≈ ≈ ≈

When things aren't going the way you'd like, you've only got a few choices. Let's **review** what you can do:

- Give up and learn to live with things as they are;
- Blame the rest of the world for your woes;
- Stick to the way you've been doing things in the hope that the world will change; or
- Change the way you've been doing things.

Since you're reading this book, the fourth choice must make the most sense to you. You've decided you're willing to explore new and different ways of doing things.

What you want to change is up to you. It could be something in your personal life, or it may be something at work. Let's start with the professional side of things for a moment. Let me begin by introducing you to the concept of *contradiction*. If you're in sales and are afraid to call on customers, that's a contradiction between your goal (improved sales) and the conditions under which you're trying to achieve that goal. For you to succeed, you will need to **remove the contradiction**. In this case, the primary contradiction is the **fear** of calling on customers. A **second contradiction** results from the human tendency to **avoid the unpleasant** (even if the unpleasant is necessary) by finding other things to do, in other words, by finding a **distraction**. In this case, both contradictions— the fear and the distraction—are standing in the way of the goal. How do you remove them?

Let's attack the distractions, first. There was a case several years ago wherein a young man answered an ad for telephone work. When the young man went for the interview, he was told that the work meant calling people on the phone. He agreed and accepted the job. At the end of his first week, however, he had made very few calls. Instead, he'd arranged, rearranged, and arranged yet again the pencils, pads, pens, paper clips, and rubber bands on his desk. He'd made endless notes and began each day recopying the ones he'd made the day before. Finally, confronted by his supervisor, the fellow confessed that he was afraid to call people on the phone. The young man was fired.

To avoid this sort of drastic resolution to a fairly common problem, the young man needed to remove everything from the desk but the phone. The paper, lunch plans, or other tasks he had in his line of vision were keeping him from achieving his goals.

The next thing he needed to do was to start making calls. Sure, the first few would likely go badly. But that's a problem with technique. And, his technique couldn't be improved until he got past the fear and discomfort he associated with making calls. The fear and discomfort had to be addressed first.

Let's use another example. Most people don't like

getting inoculations. For most of us, our first memory of going to the doctor's office was a fear of getting a shot. Even adults, while they may no longer yell, scream or hide under the doctor's examination table, generally do not like getting shots; they merely hide it better than children do.

Yet we also know that thousands of people are required to give themselves injections of insulin or other medications. Do these people enjoy the experience, particularly when they first begin? Probably not. But they do it anyway because they have to. Their lives, literally, depend upon it. In time, the experience, while never pleasant, loses much, if not all, of the mental discomfort associated with it.

Do you remember the first time you attempted to dive off the high board at the local pool? Remember how high it seemed? Remember your first dance, how it looked and felt like everyone but you knew what to do? Staying home and avoiding the dance didn't solve the problem and neither did standing in a corner all night.

This concept, whether it's about making sales calls, diving off high boards, or striking up a conversation with strangers at a conference, is essentially the same: **Do what you fear until you fear it no more**.

So, for the person afraid to make sales calls, that initial contradiction between goal and condition, that fear of making sales calls, must be overcome because that's the only way he or she will make money. As a second step, the distractions must be removed. All the details, all the applications, all the documents, and sharpened pencils are secondary to being in front of people to make money. That must remain the focus. Remember, as we have said before, the achievement of a well-formed outcome is the goal.

A good friend of mine is a political consultant. When he approaches a new campaign or teaches others how to run successful political campaigns, he accents three central concepts that I think apply here. These are the *target*, the *strategy* and the *tactics*. The *target* he defines as winning 50 percent plus one of the total votes cast. The *strategy* is winning the votes of certain specific groups or areas. The *tactics* may be direct mail pieces, TV or radio ads, or the other tools he uses to win those votes.

Similarly, we may think of the well-formed outcome as the target. Next, we need to devise strategies for achieving that outcome. Finally, we need to identify and implement successful tactics to bring these strategies to fruition.

These are the three first steps towards achieving a well-formed outcome. In the case we have been discussing, the target is increased sales. The successful sales call is an obvious strategy towards achieving that goal. The initially identified tactic is the removal of the existing contradictions between conditions and that goal. Additional tactics for the salesperson, such as improving his or her knowledge of the products and client base will follow as he or she overcomes the initial obstacles of call avoidance and distractions.

Let's take another example. Imagine you want and truly believe that you deserve a promotion. You have come to the conclusion that your current supervisor will be of no help in this endeavor because he or she has no promotions to offer, because he or she resents you and is not willing to see you do well, because he or she is content in his or her current position and thinks everyone else ought to be similarly content in theirs, or for whatever other reason might exist.

The goal or target is realistic, theoretically attainable and at least partially within your power to achieve. **Step one complete**.

Step two, the strategy, requires that we analyze current conditions. If you follow the Clueless methodology, you might march into Mr. Stuffenbottom's office, demand a promotion, and threaten to quit if you don't get it. The Cardless Card Trick, on the other hand, suggests that you first **think** about which conditions favor your outcome, and which do not.

Among the conditions favoring the achievement of your goal are the facts that you do your job very well. You also have several ideas, which, you believe, will enhance the company's chances for overall success. Conditions not in your favor, however, include the fact that no one in the chain of command above your immediate supervisor seems to know that you are doing a good job. In fact, no one in the chain of command above your immediate supervisor seems to know that you even exist. So, one strategy might be getting these people to know who you are. **Step two at least partially complete**.

Now, step three: tactics. How to get them to take notice of you becomes the issue. You can all but guarantee that you'd be noticed if you ran naked through the company's reception area or came to work with a banana sticking out of each ear, but that is probably not the type of attention you want. It could be, however, that for a variety of reasons you have avoided or not taken advantage of opportunities that do exist for coming into contact with those above your supervisor in the chain of command. There are lots of opportunities for making such contact: the company golf outing, picnic, charitable event, fundraiser or advanced training program. I knew of one woman who, upon hearing that an Elks lodge was sponsoring a charitable breakfast on behalf of a local Scout troop, attended because she knew her boss' boss was a ranking member of the lodge and would likely be there. He was and she was able to use the low-pressure, off-site opportunity to talk with him and make a favorable impression.

But this brings us to, or perhaps brings us back to, how we see ourselves. Way back, when we described your "nice" meeting her "nice," in the section on dating and the difference between formal and informal behavior (revisit Chapter 3 in case you forgot), we pointed out that it takes a while before the person hiding behind the "nice" comes out. Along those lines, we also discussed the concepts of the self and the person. Inherent in both of these discussions was the notion that there is a division within most of us, a separation between who we really are and who we want the outside world to think we are. Clark Kent and Superman, Bruce Wayne and Batman. Two sides of the same person. Let's call this a *duality*.

At the risk of muddying the waters even more, I'm going to suggest that there is another duality we should examine, maybe even a duality within a duality.

If we accept the concepts of self and person, we also have to recognize that somewhere embedded in one of those two sides is a self-image. The problem is that if we believe our self-image actually resides in the self-portion of our being, then we probably have to accept that the person may be phony. Conversely, if we truly associate our self-image with the person we project to the outside world that might suggest that we don't really think much of the self we really are. Why is this important? I think it is basic to the successful design of the well-formed outcome.

We spoke earlier of the concept of contradiction, a disparity between what we're trying to achieve and the

MIRROR, MIRROR ON THE WALL...

conditions in which we're trying to achieve it. Just as we tell our kids that they can't successfully do their home-work, study, and get anything out of the exercise if they are doing it in front of a blaring TV, we have to take a seri-ous look at the contradictions that are not only standing in the way of our achieving our well-formed outcomes, but might very well be standing in the way of those out-comes being well-formed in the first place.

Earlier, we defined a realistic version of a well-formed outcome as realistic, attainable, and something over which we have some measure of control. But wouldn't you agree that a well-formed outcome is also something that will make us happy? And beyond mak-ing us happy, I would suggest that it should be truly well formed; the outcome should also be something that is good for us, something beneficial that won't ultimately turn around and bite us once we've attained it.

Perhaps an unfortunate but thoroughly recogniza-ble set of examples might serve to illustrate the point. I had a friend who had been married to a very good, though unexciting, woman for about eight years. He was content enough, but was convinced that he was bored. Along came a stunning 21-year-old redhead. She was exciting. She and her friends had parties; they went out dancing, they did things. It also probably helped that the young redhead fed his ego in a way that his wife no longer (if ever) did. So, my friend decided that his imme-diate well-formed outcome would be establishing a rela-tionship with the young redhead.

I'll spare you the details, but the actual outcome was a painful and messy divorce after which the young redhead ran off with someone else. In this case, well-formed is not the term I'd use to describe the outcome my friend actually achieved.

Similarly, I knew of a woman who decided that a certain promotion was her particular well-formed outcome. She designated target, strategy, and tactics like General Sherman heading to the sea. Nothing was going to stand in her way and nothing did. She achieved her goal. However, the goal, the promotion, meant relocating her family halfway across the country to a completely alien environment. To accomplish this she had to pull her kids out of schools where they were doing extremely well, her husband had to give up the job he'd worked at for almost 15 years, and the spacious house that had been their home had to be replaced by something that turned out to be more expensive but not nearly as nice. She also had to commit to traveling at least 15 or more days a month and to working late and on weekends with little, if any, down time for herself or her family. Once again, the results she achieved in the end were not much different than those achieved by my friend who chased the redhead. In several ways, they were even sadder.

Yet, in both of these cases, the individuals behind the respective chains of events really thought that the outcomes they sought truly were well-formed. The question is "**Were they?**"

In both cases, the immediate realization of the pursued goal—the redhead and the promotion, respectively—led to a sense of happiness. But, in both cases, the happiness was fleeting and the actual results of the achievement made everyone concerned decidedly less than happy. So again, we have to ask whether the desired outcomes were indeed well-formed and if not, why not?

I am going to suggest (and thereby cleverly tie up several loose ends all at the same time) that in these cases and many others we could think of, the fallacy lay in mistaking the source of the **attraction** the goals had in the first place.

We have established that we all embody a duality between our self and our person. We have also recognized that our self-image resides in one, the other, or perhaps even both of these distinct parts of who we are. But these two parts of who we are are not the same. We mentioned Superman, a familiar figure who we know is also Clark Kent—but they're not the same person. Superman is powerful, confident, strong, and brave. Clark, on the other hand, is none of these things. Clark is attracted to Lois Lane. So is Superman. She is attracted to Superman, but not to Clark. Clark continually tries to win her affection, but fails. Superman spurns her affections, in turn, because he wants her to love him for his real self, the non-Super Clark. What a mess!

We do many if not all of the things that Superman/Clark does in our relationship to the world. We show the world our confident person and accept the world's accolades, while secretly wishing that the world would accept and love our homey, homely self. This, in and of itself, causes stress in our everyday lives. But this stress can be compounded, sometimes disastrously so, when we set out to define a well-formed outcome and lose sight of which side of our being, the self or the person, we are seeking to gratify. In the two cases I just cited, my friend with the redhead and the woman seeking the big, important promotion, it was the person that was being gratified while the self was just being dragged along for the ride. And therein lay the seeds of disaster.

How do we discern between something appealing to our self and something appealing to our person?

You may notice that I haven't referred to given outcomes as ill-advised merely because they only appeal to the ego even though, in a way, I can see where one might be tempted to use that word, particularly in the two examples I used above. Clearly, the redhead appealed to my friend's ego, as did the perks and title of the big, important promotion the woman sought. But I believe this analysis is too simple. I believe that both sides of our being, both the self and the person, have an ego.

Confused?

Let's go slowly. Our overall goal is to facilitate our environment so that we can achieve our well-formed outcomes. But facilitating our environment to achieve outcomes that are not well-formed is not only a large waste of time; it can be dangerous and cause us more harm than good. To know the difference between an outcome that is truly well-formed as opposed to its often attractive but dangerously imperfect counterpart, we must have as our basis a well-formed self. This well-formed self is the result of a process that stems immediately from a self-image, itself the product of a self-evaluation that is the product of two distinct sources.

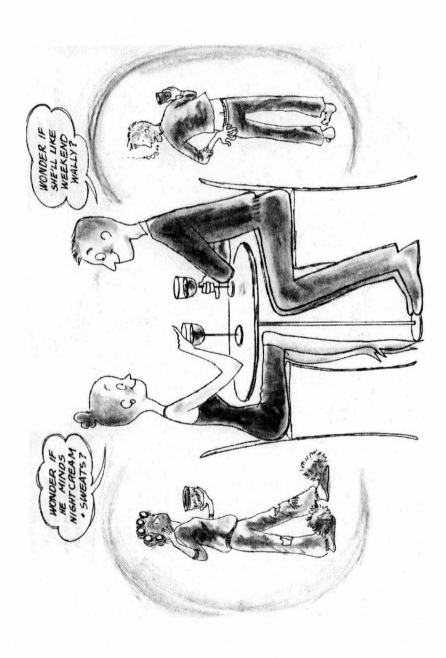

CHAPTER 14

Back to Basics

&a &a &a

Okay, so now you're really confused. I don't blame you. But it isn't really all that difficult to follow. Let's remember, as we said, that facilitating your environment is the goal here, and we want to make sure you do it for the right reasons and in the right situations. Because, if you don't, the end result will be only more frustration and stress.

An initial step is deciding upon a well-formed outcome. But we can't stop there. We have to make sure that the outcome truly is well-formed. How do we do that? By examining the source of the outcome's attraction. We have to go **back to the basics** that made you who you are.

The basic premise we're working from here is that we are all caught between conflicting images of what we feel we should be.

Let's take my friend with the redhead for an example again. He was probably taught by family, teachers, and church that he should be a good and faithful husband. But Madison Avenue, Hollywood, *Playboy Magazine*, and our culture at large also imparted the message that he should have a pretty, exciting, young woman on his arm if he was going to be a real man. Similarly, he might have felt that he should be faithful to his wife and also felt that he had some sort of right to the pretty, young redhead (no wonder he was so messed up!).

Where, we have to ask, did these conflicting teachings and feelings come from? Let's go back a bit and try to find an answer.

In earlier pages we discussed how your person and your self are the products of your genetic make-up and outside influences. Remember when you filled out the answers to those questions? That exercise was designed to help you sort through some of these outside influences. What might some of the influences have been?

Your parents were certainly primary outside influences. So were your siblings, if you had any. Your extended family, your boyfriends or girlfriends and their parents, your teachers, and your overall circumstances were all part of these outside influences.

Somewhere along the line, however, not all the messages these outside influences bombarded you with settled into the same sort of foundation. The filter of your genetic personality let some through into a deeper level while the others remained, still there, but a step removed from your innermost being. This was the beginning of the differentiation between your self and your person.

As this process evolved, therefore, some notions, concepts, likes, and dislikes became more deeply embedded within you. You discovered that while you liked ice cream, as almost everyone does, you preferred vanilla to chocolate. You came to realize that while you could listen to the rock music all your friends liked, you really liked country or folk. You discovered that you actually did have distinct preferences in clothes, make-up, and entertainment.

But at the same time, you were eager to be popular, to fit in, to have a budding romance or two. You began to see the wider world beyond your familiar childhood environment. You begin to see possibilities out there for you.

As this happened, you somehow survived your teenage and young adult years. We commonly hear of young people needing to find themselves. What they are going through, and what you and I have already gone through with varying degrees of success and failure, is the initial separation and later synthesis of the self-generated self-image and the environmentally generated self-image.

The self-generated self-image comes from those influences that get through the filter of our genetically stamped personality and take deep root in our inner being. The environmentally generated self-image forms the rest of what we understand to be the **"rules of the game"** if we are to succeed in the society into which we have been born. Now, this is an important point, for as we have said before, culture and society dictate those rules and our understanding of them. Americans, for example, are raised to prize individuality. The Japanese, by contrast, stress much greater conformity. Thus, an American child who truly doesn't want to stand out may feel that he or she is a failure, while the strong-willed little girl born into a Japanese family may grow up thinking herself an embarrassment to her parents.

Children, as we have noted, are born a blank tablet onto which is etched what we have come to popularly call a personality. Initially, children have no concept of self. This forms and changes over the years. These are the years during which the child, bombarded by outside or environmental influences, filters some in and takes those few as his or her own. Yet the child must also learn how to fit into the society around her. She must learn what is expected of her and how to function. For this information, she relies upon those environmental influences that she has retained all along. Still, there is very often a conflict between the ones she has truly made her own and the rest.

Thus, as the self-image forms, it is, from the very start, shaped by two distinct sources: the values and messages that have gotten through the genetic personality filter and those still bombarding her from the outside environment.

The growing child sifts through these, measures and weighs them against each other. This is self-evaluation, the basic analysis of "Who am I?" But it also gives rise to "Who am I supposed to be?"

The answer is measured yet again. The result is a self-image, a synthesis . . . and very often a built-in conflict.

As we stated above, defining well-formed outcomes is nearly impossible unless a well-formed self is the basis of the decision. Why? Because the inherent danger is mistaking those environmentally generated influences upon us for the self-generated ones at the core of our being. The inability to differentiate between these two very real sources of attraction and impulse can lead to ill-formed outcomes, which we pursue as though they were well-formed. The results can be disastrous.

In the next chapter we will discuss a few final concepts to wrap the threads of this discussion together. They are the *shaping pattern, individuation, the currency of approval* and *defining rites of passage.* From this we will turn to concepts of the Leader Within You and whether such concepts will lead you to where you want to be.

CHAPTER 15

Have I Told You Lately. . . .

ᕷ ᕷ ᕷ

There are several additional concepts we need to discuss. Each of these concepts represents a distinct step in the formation of your person and self. Why do some of us pursue ill-formed outcomes, play Clueless, fatally combine authority figures, and get stuck in an "I must/but I can't" mindset that leads to frustration? Let's examine some of the life choices we have made, consciously or otherwise, that have led to patterns of either acquiescence to or rejection of the norms, goals, and rules we encounter in life. And let's call this the *shaping pattern*.

The parts or facets of this pattern are *individuation*, *the currency of approval*, and *defining rites of passage*, which we are about to discuss.

Let's begin with the shaping pattern. Recall the example of the potter who molds something beautiful from raw clay. Imagine once again that we begin, as does that raw clay. There are different kinds of clay and each possesses different properties. Experienced potters know the difference, even though you and I only see lumps of mud.

In much the same way, a roomful of babies probably looks much the same to the outside observer. Some babies may be a bit cuter than the rest, but if we have no chance to interact with any of them and are observing them through a window, like in a maternity ward, we cannot tell one child from another. Just as with the potter's clay, other than one baby looking darker than another, there is, to the viewer, no significant difference between these babies.

We would not, for example, know which had inherited genes for a talent in music, which would want to draw from the minute she could hold a pencil. We would not know which would be a natural athlete, which would gravitate towards politics, mathematics, business or psychotherapy. We would not know which child had inherited an independent nature and which one was naturally passive. We would not know which of these children already had the genes that made him susceptible to cancer, being overweight or any other genetically inherited characteristic. But each of these children, just like the potter's clay, would have the distinct characteristics whether we could see them or not.

Several years later, we'd notice that some are better dressed than others. Some are showing alarming signs of future obesity. Others look downright undernourished. We'd observe that one little girl stutters. Three of the children seem to have a surprising vocabulary for their ages, while several are already displaying the language of the streets, their speech sprinkled with vernacular and slang.

We still don't know these kids, but from these observations we'd be able to make a few educated guesses as to the paths upon which these children have been placed. We can guess that some were born to a parent or parents who are willing and able to provide them with good, caring homes. Others were not. We can see that this one or that one comes from a home with more money than one or two of the others. In other words, we're already seeing, even at this tender age, the signs of the shaping pattern, the molding of these children, into the adults they will be someday.

So it was with each of us. The homes, families, communities, and social settings into which each of us was born began shaping us almost immediately. And, from our earliest days, a differentiation set in between aspects of this overall shaping pattern which would eventually be the basis of our self and our person.

For the child, much of this is an unconscious process. The little girl is aware that she likes one food more than another, maybe likes one color more than another, likes pants as opposed to dresses, or likes "boy" toys better than "girl" toys. But until the age of about eight, these preferences are not largely interpreted by her as being the beginnings of a distinct personality. Why? Because in the early years of life we have little need for a distinct personality.

This is not to say that children growing up with siblings, especially twins do not have a need to differentiate themselves from their brothers and sisters. But for the young child, this is most often expressed in terms of who he or she is not, as opposed to who he or she is. In other words, a child, particularly a younger child in a family, may not want to follow the lead of his or her older brother or sister. This child may fight to have things his way in any given situation. But this is different than truly having a sense of self.

"We're having pasta for supper," you may tell a child.

The child may reply, "I don't want pasta for supper."

"OK," you may reply, "then what do you want?"

Here the child's logic often breaks down. He or she may name a sweet or a dessert or something that is impossible to prepare. Or he or she may simply say, "I don't know, just not pasta."

The point is that the child's assertion of individuality is merely a claim to be not Mom, not Dad, not Sis or Big Brother, all of whom are perfectly content with having pasta for supper. Perhaps we should call this a sort of proto-individuation, a forerunner of the real thing that will come later.

However, by the time a child reaches sixth grade, individuation has finally begun. What is **individuation**? There is a breaking away from the patterns and bonds that largely defined earlier life. As the parent of any middle-school child knows well, this is the stage when children begin to assert the fact that they like certain styles of clothes, music, and entertainment. It is the point when they begin to see friends as important. It is the point when kids begin to develop outside interests in sports, scouting or a hobby.

To understand this process, we must go back to the lumps of clay again. We have already made the point that newborn children lack not only a sense of self, but also a sense of desire. They do have a sense of want, in terms of food, comfort, and love. They do not understand these wants on any sort of intellectual level, but they do know when they're hungry, wet, cold, uncomfortable or in pain. They do know that they want to be close to Mommy, held or played with by Daddy. They do know that they want to be loved. But this want, this hard-wired impulse we are all born with is not the same as desire, which is more of a cognitive process.

Desire is harder to pin down. The thing desired often does not fill an immediate need, it is often not physically present at the moment, and the pleasure it represents can be anticipated. In other words, the ability to desire is formed as the individual grows, learns, and experiences. The impulse to want, on the other hand, is innate and has several very specific points of focus. As we've mentioned, one of these is the fact that the child wants the love of his or her parents.

But how does the child measure this love? Clearly, it is at least partially measured by the physical affection a parent shows a child. The child wants to be held, snuggled, kissed, and made to feel safe. Beyond this, the child wants to be told he is loved.

But as a child reaches the ages of three, four, and five, the child begins to look for something else. He wants to be told that he is a good boy; she wants to be told that she has done something well. Are these children seeking love? Yes, and no.

In an unconscious way, the child has gone beyond asking simply, "Do you love me?" and is now asking, "Do you like me?" The child has already come to accept that the parent's love will continue to be there. In fact, the child's assumption is that the parent's love will always be there. So, while the child still wants to be told that he or she is loved now and again, another need has come into the picture, the desire for approval.

The child's innate need for love has not gone away. But even at this early stage of life that love has become one of the child's operating assumptions. In other words, it is not something the child feels he or she needs to reestablish each day. But a parent's approval is another matter entirely.

Consider the frequency with which a young child

of two or three requires discipline and then cries. Why does she cry? Clearly, the child is experiencing some level of frustration at not getting her way. But beyond that, the child probably fears that the reprimand, harsh voice, punishment, or spank on the bottom means that she has lost her parent's love. What does the parent do?

Let's go back to the question of whether it is the person or the self, which most often seeks the approval of others. I think a strong case can be made for the fact that it is the outer person, rather than the inner self, that is most gratified by or seeks the approval of others. By contrast—and to illustrate the point—let's take a look at what facet of our being benefits from either keeping our parents as our source of approval or becoming self-approving or affirming.

We have already taken it as a given that, completely dysfunctional situations aside, your parents will always love you. Further, parents have the sneaky ability, matched only by that of spouses and really good friends, of being able to see past your person to your self. In fact, this ability may be the only reason they (along with spouses and really good friends) can love you in the first place. So, once you've gotten past the three- and four-year-old stage where you need the approval of Mommy or Daddy for your affirmation, what does that approval get you that you do not already have?

As a child it is important to realize that Mommy and Daddy like you as well as love you. But as an adult, being secure in their love, their liking you is simply icing on the cake. It is an extra connection that in reality pales in comparison with the love you already receive from them. And since it's your self with which your parents usually interact ("You may be a hard-boiled CEO to everyone else, but you'll always be my little girl to me."),

HEY MOM + DAD, LOOK AT ME.

the approval of your parents would not seem to have much luster for your outer-directed person.

So if the approval of parents speaks primarily to the self and self-approval clearly speaks to the self, what of the approval of others? Why do we adopt others—peers, bosses or society at large—as our source of approval? Because the approval of others speaks largely (if not exclusively) to our already outer-directed person.

The person is the shell within which the self lives. The person interacts with most of the people with whom we come into contact. Outsiders give their approval to the person, not to the self.

When Mr. Stuffenbottom gets angry with you, the assistant manager, he is not angry with your self; he is not saying that you are an awful person and have no worth as a human being. He's saying that (at the moment) he thinks you have no worth as an assistant manager. Conversely, when ol' Stuffenbottom applauds your performance, has you featured in the company newsletter, and rewards you with a brand new box of paperclips, he is not applauding your inner self. You could be Mother Teresa or Lucretia Borgia in your private life; Stuffenbottom neither knows nor cares. All he knows is that you're a damned good assistant manager and you did a bang-up job on the latest project for the firm's largest account. So which side of your being, the self or the person, is basking in his approval or, conversely, wishing you had it?

Did the girls in your junior high school clique care more about whether you read to your sight-impaired grandmother last night or whether you shared their taste in music? Did the guys you hung out with in high school care more about whether you helped your father paint the family room or whether you could get the car on

Friday night? Do your co-workers care more about whether you finished your portion of a departmental project or whether you volunteered the past several nights at the local soup kitchen? Are the guys on the golf course more impressed with the way you handled that large account or the way you taught the Scout troop to tie a square knot?

Each of these examples points to the desire of seeking the approval of others and highlights a major observation. As we each enter the stage of individuation we seem to need to find new sources of approval.

Ideally, we should rely on a mixture of sources for the approval we need and desire. Yes, the approval of others is important in our lives. It is certainly important in our professional lives and can be important in our private lives as well. But we must also recognize that, since the approval of others is generally focused towards our outer-directed person, our inner-self can and will suffer if others become our sole or primary source of approval and affirmation.

There is a difference between a well-formed outcome and its misshapen, mutant cousin, the ill-formed outcome. Recall that we differentiated between the two on the basis of whether the result was good for us, or only appeared that way at first. Think back to the example of my friend with the young redhead. Was she a well-formed outcome? Was the messy, painful, and humiliating divorce that followed that chain of events a well-formed outcome? Was my friend's **"self"** enhanced in any way by all this? Or was his **"person"** merely gratified by the approving leers of his buddies at the bar when he sashayed in with the comely size six on his arm?

Would he not have been better off had he been able to rely upon an inner sense of approval in himself, a sense that could have better evaluated what he had, what he might lose or how else he could have delivered a message to his wife that he was unhappy? Instead, he chose to meet a need within his self, through his person.

So we see that even in the initial stages of individuation we sow the seeds of later conflict and frustration. Yes, individuation moves us physically and emotionally away from the primary source of approval upon which we relied as a child. And this is, as it ought to be. Going through life with the umbilical cord still attached is no way to fulfill yourself or your potential. But allowing yourself to become completely other directed, to gauge your worth based upon the approval of others, is to allow the essential shaping process to take a drastically wrong turn. Not only do we risk losing the affection of those truly important to us, but also we run the risk of becoming so directed toward gratifying our person that our self suffers long-term damage.

Exercise:

(CHILD) SELF	(CHILD) PERSON
TYPES OF APPROVAL	TYPES OF APPROVAL
————————————	————————————
————————————	————————————
————————————	————————————

(ADULT) SELF

TYPES OF APPROVAL

———————————————

———————————————

———————————————

(ADULT) PERSON

TYPES OF APPROVAL

———————————————

———————————————

———————————————

CHAPTER 16

Glory Days

ða ða ða

We've discussed the fact that, as we grow from childhood to adulthood, we shift our sources of approval. In other words, we go from being the child who relies upon his parents' approval to give him a sense of affirmation, to the adolescent, teenager, and, finally, the adult who has the ability to consciously replace the approval he sought from his parents with the approval of others whose opinion he now deems important. But is this approval signaled in the same ways over time? Is there, or should there be, a differentiation in the form that approval takes?

There is a distinct difference between the ways approval is given and the ways we look for it. I call this the *currency of approval*.

We are all familiar with the world's major currencies: the American dollar, the British pound, the Euro dollar, and so on. Each has an intrinsic value in its specific location. Russian black markets aside, you need British pounds to purchase something in England, yen to buy something in Japan, and dollars to pay a debt in America.

So, too, in the market of approval, there are currencies specific to our stage of life. Our changing levels of maturity and our chronological age dictate these currencies. This is important because we need to recognize that there are different ways by which we measure whether we have the approval we seek, differences determined by our relationships or by the settings in which we are seeking that approval.

The parent who wants to show approval for something his five-year-old has done will likely give the child a hug, say "Good boy" and perhaps tell the child what a big boy he is becoming. This is sufficient for the child, who leaves the encounter with a glow of satisfaction, the knowledge of his parent's approval, and a strengthened sense of affirmation.

But as we grow older, these signs of approval are no longer sufficient for our internal needs. In fact, if those kinds of approval were all we received, we would feel ill used in many cases. When you finally subdue that tough customer in tough negotiations and win the coveted account, how are you looking for ol' Stuffenbottom to react? Are you looking for him to pat you on the head and say, "Good boy"? Are you looking for a hug? No! You want something tangible: a raise, a promotion, and a bigger office. More to the point, if you don't receive any of these things, you will feel ill used, no matter how effusive Stuffenbottom is in his approval.

We discussed a situation similar to this in an earlier section. We noted at that time that your anticipation of further reward could have been a faulty operating presumption. But, for argument's sake this time, let us imagine that Stuffenbottom had let it be known that there'd be big things in store for the account executive who landed that difficult account. So, this time, the anticipation of reward is not being fueled merely by an operating assumption. It is being fueled by what everyone interprets as Stuffenbottom's promise.

So how do you define what the big things Stuffenbottom mentioned might be? Given the currency of approval in the modern business world, you would naturally assume that a raise, a bonus, a promotion, an executive parking spot or a new office might be appropriate representations of Stuffenbottom's pleasure. Somehow, the extra half hour of television that your parents might have rewarded you with when you were seven years old would not quite suffice in this situation. So, if Stuffenbottom merely rewards you with "Good boy!" you feel cheated.

Let's take a real-life example. I knew a woman who was an only child and had been the sole focus of her doting parents' constant and effusive praise. Attending a small grammar school, she was the teachers' favorite, in no small part because she was an exceptional student. At college, she not only routinely made the dean's list, but also took several honors and graduated, with much pomp and circumstance, at the top of her class.

Between her excellent grades and a few lucky connections, she was among the first in her class to land a job upon graduation. While her classmates were still busy sending out resumes, she had already begun working in the biochemistry lab of a well-known New York City hospital.

In a very short time, however, she was unhappy. Within less than a year, she quit the job and returned to school for a graduate degree. Within two years, a master's degree under her belt, she was again working in a lab, somewhere near Boston. Four months later, she left the job and was at Yale pursuing a doctorate.

Well, you might say, there's nothing wrong with pursuing higher education. Perhaps she was readying herself for a better position than those she had previously been offered. That could be, but the odd thing was that she wasn't happy at Yale either. Part of this was due to the fact that while she was still living on a grad student's stipend, her former classmates' budding careers were providing them with BMWs and vacations to the tropics. But there was more at play.

At least part of the problem was that this young lady, for all of her unquestionable intelligence, had somehow failed to realize that as she grew, the currencies of approval in her life would change over time.

Think about this. Throughout her formative years, this young lady was the sole object of the doting approval of her aged parents and their equally aged and doting friends. Throughout grammar school, high school, and even college, she received regular reinforcement of her sense of worth, whether this came in the form of her parents' bragging and doting, the "Ooos and Ahs" of her parents' friends, the recognition she regularly received from teachers or even the various certificates she received in high school and college. Then suddenly she found herself in the real world of employment. Suddenly there were no more "Oooos." Suddenly there were no more "Ahs." There were no more gold stars on the top of her papers, no more assemblies in which she was awarded a certificate for having the highest marks in the class. No more dean's list.

To her supervisors, she was another bright, young college graduate who had to start at the bottom and work her way up. When she successfully completed running her blood chemistries, no one patted her on the head. No one told her how bright she was. And no one bragged about her to visitors to the lab.

Unhappy, she returned to school where interactions with her professors provided a measure of gratification. But upon returning to the work world, she was unhappy again. Finally, she wound up at Yale. Here she was not the smartest or the brightest. Here, again, no one made a fuss over her. Here, again, she was unhappy.

Part of her problem was that she had not yet let go of the yearning for approval she had become accustomed to earlier in her life. She did not recognize that as she grew the **currencies of approval had changed**. So for her to expect the same type of recognition from her supervisors that she received from her parents created a frustrated and conflicted young woman.

Do you recall the Tom Hanks movie "Big"? In this film Hanks plays a little boy who suddenly wakes up one day as a grown man. He finds his way to the offices of a toy manufacturer and there amazes everyone with his knowledge of what sort of toys kids really like. The bosses reward him with a job and a big office. But he's not interested in the big office; he only wants to play with the toys.

To me, this has always been a classic illustration of the different currencies of approval with which we are rewarded in the various stages and situations of our lives. The Hanks character saw no value in the rewards his bosses at the toy company were bestowing upon him; he was still looking for the sort of rewards he valued as a child.

As we grow and develop, as the relationships in which we find ourselves grow and develop, the currencies of approval change as well. For many of us, this is not an easy transition to make, mentally or emotionally. While we may agree that, on the surface, the concept is self-evident, we nonetheless find ourselves stuck some-

where between evolving personal and professional relationships and the unmet desire for currencies of approval that are no longer entirely appropriate to the moment.

Let's review for a moment to get a better sense of why this is important. We have established that who you are is largely a product of the shaping patterns you experienced as you grew to adulthood. Chief among these shaping patterns is the process of individuation. You began to establish your distinct personality. You chose new sources of approval. And you were rewarded with a changing set of currencies of approval. Just as your parents probably never told you that you were the "coolest," that statement was, by contrast, the sort of comment—a currency of approval—you sought from your friends in junior high school. Similarly, where the high school coach may have slapped you on the butt while congratulating you for the fantastic touchdown catch you made, you'd probably be a bit put off if Stuffenbottom slapped your butt in a staff meeting.

Where a girlfriend in high school or on spring break in college may have remarked on her envy at your success with boys, it would not be appropriate for your division supervisor to make a similar comment concerning your luck with men.

"Okay, Mark," you might be saying, "I realize that it isn't appropriate for Stuffenbottom to smack my butt as a token of his approval. But, on the other hand, I don't want him to. **What's your point?**"

My point is this: While we may all recognize that Stuffenbottom should keep his hands to himself, and further recognize that the example is a bit silly, there are many situations in life in which our dissatisfaction comes from looking for a form or currency of approval that is either no longer appropriate to our stage in life or no longer appropriate to the situation.

The boss, for example, is probably not going to make a fuss over you every time you do something right. Your mother may have, the teachers at school may have, the coach may have—but the boss isn't likely to.

In the Bruce Springstein song, "Glory Days," the subject is a group of people who long for the glory days of high school, the days of football heroics, and being the prettiest girl in the class. More to the point, I think we all know at least one or two people who could have been characters in that song. Whether these people are stuck in high school, college, the '60s, their twenties or any other time in their lives, they seem to truly miss the glory of that period—and the currencies of approval that went with it.

The woman who misses her days as the reigning prom queen and their rewards, but somehow overlooks the absolute love her children show her, and the man who continually rehashes the glory days of his college football career, but overlooks the trust his boss places in him with increasingly more important assignments are two examples of people yearning for the wrong currency of approval.

Think about how often we hear people we know complaining that the spark has gone out of their marriages? How often do we hear a man complaining that before he and his wife got married, their sex life was fantastic, but that now she just doesn't seem all that interested any more? How often do we hear women complain that their husbands were once attentive and now can't even seem to remember their anniversary? Is the spark really gone? Or is the affection just being shown in different ways? Is the approval of the spouse truly gone, or has the currency of that approval changed?

The wife of the complaining husband might point out that while it may be true that she no longer greets him at the door with a glass of champagne, Sade on the stereo, the scented oil lamps lit in the bedroom and practically nothing on, it is also true that she is a full-time mother to their three children, has a job, has stuck with him through thick and thin (including the 15 months when he was unemployed), and does her best to make sure that his home is as comfortable as it can be.

And, in similar fashion, the husband who can't seem to remember anniversaries might point out that he tries to help his wife by cooking at least three meals a week for the family, that he not only manages to get his dirty underwear in the hamper but actually does the family wash on weekends, has volunteered as an adult leader with their daughters' Girl Scout troop, has never cheated on her in 20 years of marriage, and never fails to remember to put the toilet seat back down.

These actions are valid currencies of approval. They might not be the flowers that were once sent for no reason at all, they might not be the "afternoon delight" that used to consume languid afternoons. But they are nonetheless valid and should be appreciated.

Finally, we should take note of the fact that in longing for past currencies of approval we often put a shine on a past that wasn't actually all that shiny. Let's take the young woman at Yale, for example. She may indeed have missed the doting of her parents, but she is also forgetting the suffocating way they overprotected her that nearly caused her to leave home. The woman complaining that her husband no longer sends her flowers as he used to may be overlooking the fact that many of those bouquets were, in fact, peace offerings to atone for something stupid, boneheaded or plain immature he had done. And the man who complains that his wife no longer has that spark may similarly be forgetting the frustrating girl she used to be before she matured into the unshakable mate he now has by his side.

I remember an episode of the Twilight Zone about a man, overwhelmed with the pressures of life, who became increasingly fixated upon the old neighborhood, games, and playmates of his youth. Endlessly recounting games of ring-a-leeveo, (a New York City game of tag), stickball, and the like, he slipped farther and farther away from reality. He kept asking, "**Why can't it be like it used to be?**"

Finally, in true Twilight Zone fashion, he became a boy again, playing on the streets of the Lower East Side. And what he discovered was that the neighborhood wasn't as charming as he remembered; it was dirty and dangerous. He discovered that the games he recalled had never actually been to his liking because he'd been excluded. And he learned that those he remembered, as friends had, in fact, been bullies who only let him tag along when he had money they could spend. In short, he learned that the past wasn't all that rosy and that the currencies of approval he thought he missed could no longer make him happy. In fact, they may never have made him happy.

Sure, when your picture appeared in the local newspaper back when you were ten, it was fun. Everyone from the milkman to the barber saw it and commented on it. The currency of approval was appropriate for that time, the setting, and your age; you basked in the glow of the whole community's notice. However, that does not necessarily mean that if you have an article published in the paper today that everyone or anyone is going to read it, remember to mention it, or call you on the phone with congratulations.

Does that mean that no one cares? Probably not. What it means is that for the currencies of approval appropriate to you today, just getting the article published should be enough; however, many times we go looking for others to give us the approval we seek.

The boss is not your mother. Your co-workers are not the circle of friends with whom you spent almost every waking moment of your childhood; your lives are tangential to each other only at work. Your co-workers, therefore, are probably not going to make a fuss over your piece in the paper.

Is this bad? No. **It's change**.

Look at it this way. Just as individuation helped us break away from our parents and establish ourselves as people in our own right, just as new sources of approval and evolving currencies of approval moved us from parents to friends, from friends to the opposite sex and eventually to careers, families and responsibilities, so, too, did this process take something away on the other side. It took away our parents' children. They blinked and we were adults.

We cannot go back to the way things used to be any more than our parents can have their little girl or little boy back. We cannot expect the affirmations of the past, the currencies of approval in our life, to be unaltered by time.

We live; we evolve; we change. What matters is how we handle the changes.

❧ ❧ ❧

CHAPTER 17

Go West, Young Man

≈ ≈ ≈

In the past several chapters we have discussed some of the processes, the forces if you will, that helped shape you. We discussed individuation, sources of approval, and currencies of approval. We discussed the influences your environment had upon you and the way the filter of your hard-wired personality sifted through these many influences to enable you to differentiate between the concepts that appealed to your self and those your person needs to succeed in society. But is the sum of these processes all that made you the person you are? Does it represent all you can be?

The answer, I believe, is "**No, probably not**."

Somewhere along the line, as has been true throughout the history of human culture, there are certain **rites of passage, defining moments** that separate who you might have been before their occurrence from who you might be after they occur. To appreciate these demarcations in our lives, we must first understand that some are symbolic, some are physical, some are openly acknowledged, and some are private. Some of these rites

of passage impact our personal lives, some our professional lives. But each is a milestone; for better or worse,
and each can, in its own way, help define who we are.

The most basic of these lines of demarcation are
between our childhood selves and our adult selves. This
delineation is basic to every human culture and has been
in every age. Many Native American tribes, for example,
had an ordeal of one sort or another that a young man
had to undergo before he could be accepted into the adult
world of hunting and warfare. Some were tests of
strength; some were tests of courage, endurance or skill.
But all were also tests of **character**. In some tribes, the
taking of a new name further symbolized the new adult
the young man had become when his ordeal was successfully completed.

In other cultures, only a symbolic ceremony
marked the passage from childhood to adulthood.
Several African tribes used circumcision to mark this passage. In Judaism, the Bar Mitzvah or Bat Mitzvah marks
the passage for a boy or girl, respectively, from the status
of a child to one who has reached the age of legal maturity and thereby becomes obligated to observe all the
Commandments and to participate in the religious life of
the community as an adult. The Roman Catholic Church
marks this step with Confirmation, recognition that the
child has achieved adulthood and understands the concepts of sin and free will.

These symbolic passages are important to all cultures because they denote the acceptance of both duties
and privileges. If science fiction is any guide, they are not
likely to fade away: even Mr. Spock had to undergo the
Kahs'wan, Vulcan's Rite of Passage.

But these older forms of symbolism also have
modern counterparts. Some passages are legal, such as

the requirement that young men in the United States register with the Selective Service Administration upon turning 18. Entering high school, particularly in our American culture, is certainly one such milestone. Getting one's driver's license, being old enough to vote, entering college or the military (and perhaps moving away from home for the first time), and reaching the legal drinking age are all similar public manifestations of increased maturity.

Of a more private (and universal) nature are the milestones of puberty, with the physical and emotional changes and the differences in perspective they bring about. But we should not believe that once a person has reached these milestones, crossed these bridges, that the rites of passage are complete. There are many more to come and many are increasingly more difficult to recognize for what they truly are.

In the first chapter of this book we remarked that just as it was rather silly of the Wizard of Oz to give the Cowardly Lion a medal and then tell him to go be brave, it is equally silly for a priest, minister or rabbi to join a couple in wedlock and then tell them (or expect them to) go act married. In similar fashion, it is also somewhat silly and shortsighted for anyone (ourselves included) to expect us to suddenly become mature, reasonable adults simply because we have passed a symbolic, social or legal milestone of adulthood. There is more to it than that, particularly since so many modern milestones of adulthood are purely symbolic. Look at it this way: Is the immature goofball any more likely to become mature and responsible just because he is of age to get a driver's license or can (finally) buy his beer legally? Is the young woman who has become sexually active and perhaps gone on the pill suddenly imbued with the maturity to recognize a lout when she sees one and steer clear of him? Unfortunately, in both cases, the answer is no.

But even as we recognize the fact that a driver's license, a draft card or a prescription for the pill is not any guarantee of maturity, so too should we recognize that our modern society has made it particularly hard for real maturity to be achieved as it once might have been.

Horace Greeley is popularly credited with having given the advice, "**Go west, young man**" (although the truth is that Greeley borrowed that line from an Indiana editorialist named John Soule). But what was Greeley talking about and why is it important to this discussion?

Greeley wasn't giving directions to the local Wal-Mart, that's for sure. Rather, what he was referring to was the concept that the American West of his time offered almost unlimited opportunity for a young man to break the shackles of birth, ancestry, and class and make something of himself, to prove himself. It was a rite of passage that Greeley was talking about; and it was not just the West that made this possible. It was also the time.

No one asked to see Thomas Edison's engineering diploma before he was able to tinker with his many inventions. No one demanded a certificate from Whitcomb Judson before he invented the zipper. When Cecil Booth invented the vacuum cleaner, no one asked for his resume before they decided to use his invention during the preparations for the coronation of the King of England. These are but a few examples of something that was once quite possible, but today is increasingly difficult. Today, you need a diploma. Today, you need a resume. Today, it seems, one needs resources far beyond what George de Mestral, for example, needed when he invented Velcro.

Today, there are no dragons left to slay and there

are few frontiers left where a person, man or woman, can simply show up and, using God-given talent and hard work, make the sort of mark that was once possible to make on one's own. Yes, for some extremely talented and lucky individuals (like Bill Gates), the old formula can still work. But most of us are not that talented and certainly not that lucky. So how do we prove ourselves; how do we get the sense of achievement that once came from successfully completing the quest, the ordeal or the challenge? How do we define and successfully meet the rites of passage in our lives?

To answer these questions, it might be helpful to revisit something we mentioned a moment ago. In traditional societies, we noted, the rite of passage might have been symbolized by an act or ceremony, but beyond this it often involved some real accomplishment or a concrete change between the before and the after. Perhaps part of the problem we face is that the modern rites of passage we observe or recognize require next to no real action or accomplishment and, further, do not demarcate many substantial differences between what went before and what might follow. For example, we noted that, particularly in American society, going to high school is often considered a sort of passage. But what, other than surviving to freshman age, did the student accomplish to earn this passage? Somehow, an eighth grade graduation ceremony doesn't compare with being permitted to go on the hunt. Further, other than perhaps attending classes in a new building, what is really different between the student's experience before high school and after he or she starts? There are still classes to attend, tests to take, homework to do, and rules to follow.

In many early societies, including America's rural past, getting married and having children was often all it took for a young person to establish himself or herself as an adult. Can the same be said today? Just a few generations ago, many of our grandparents and great-grandparents got married and had their first children as teenagers. Would we do the same or want our children to do the same thing today? Obviously not. Why? Well, for one thing, having sex, having a baby or even getting married is no longer all one needs in this society to truly be considered an adult. Today's world requires education, training, experience, and a career. Consciously, we mark our passages by, yes, earning the driver's license, getting a first car, achieving the legal drinking age, earning the degree, securing the first real job (those years flipping burgers in McDonald's somehow do not count as real), renting the first real apartment, and buying the bigger car and the rest of the toys. Somewhere along the line we might even get married. We have arrived.

Then why do so many of us still feel unfulfilled, not yet accomplished, somehow not yet really grown up? How can we go through all the processes of individuation, through changing sources of approval, standards of approval and currencies of approval, through the differentiation between self and person and still not be—or at least not feel—**complete**?

ès ès ès

I suggest that there are two possible answers. The first is that as people, as adults, we have an innate need to measure our progress as we go through life. Yet this progress requires some standard, some yardstick against which it can be measured. For children, birthdays often serve this purpose; with each passing year and its attendant accomplishments, the child senses her progress toward her goal of growing up. But as adults, with different standards of approval and currencies of approval, birthdays no longer mean progress toward some summit we hope to reach; if anything, they often represent milestones toward a valley we cannot escape. Either way, they are not the measures we seek. As adolescents, we might view the changes of puberty or the addition of new privileges (a learner's permit, for example) as such measures. As teenagers and young adults we have analogous measures of progress upon which we rely. But upon being fully declared adults by society—usually around the time of college graduation—such measures of progress no longer suffice. So we seek others.

If we are like most people in America's consumer culture, we begin to measure our progress—and by extension our worth and value as a person—by the job we hold, the money we earn, and the things we buy. But this is where things can get confusing. Who has grown more, progressed more, the wonderful father and husband who has been unemployed for five years or the fellow with the million-dollar portfolio to go along with his three broken marriages and the children he hardly sees or knows? Who is the success, the doctor with the flourishing practice performing cosmetic surgery on Park Avenue matrons or the sole pediatrician in a northern county of Maine, barely eking out a living-serving patients who have no other source of medical care?

Perhaps no starker example of misjudged progress can be found than in a patient I had a number of years ago. Deciding to give up on a troubled but probably salvageable marriage, she then embarked on a disastrous affair and later filed for a divorce. In counseling, I asked her how she viewed both decisions. Her reply was that both were rites of passage. It was odd, but perhaps telling, that she should answer as she did. On the one hand, one might ask from what and to what did these events mark a passage? But on the other hand, one can also discern without too much difficulty the cultural basis for her answer. Among many divorced Americans, such events truly are considered nearly universal and almost the norm and, therefore, are practically expected as what she called them: rites of passage. On television, in the movies, and in life, the divorced person is so common-place as to be completely unremarkable. Yet, despite all of this, it was also abundantly clear that, while this woman might have experienced what she considered to be rites of passage that somehow marked her as a modern woman, the experience did not leave her happy or ful-filled in any sense whatsoever. To the contrary, she was miserable.

Now, this is not to say that all rites of passage are, must be or should be pleasant experiences. The death of a parent or a spouse, for example, is not pleasant. But such deaths are also natural parts of life, a condition of our existence. In similar fashion, other rites of passage, for example being downsized out of a job or having the company or plant for which you have worked for fifteen years or more close, are not pleasant experiences. But these, too, are increasingly common experiences. Sadly, it can almost be said that losing a job is becoming an American rite of passage. But beyond this, some good can come from such an experience if we handle it proper-ly and if it opens our eyes to lessons we would have oth-erwise missed had things not changed. It should also be added that a death in the family or the closing of our employer's business are things beyond our control.

In the end, I suggest that at least part of the reason why so many of us feel unfulfilled in either our personal or professional lives is that we have grown beyond the rites of passage that were once sufficient to mark our progress through life, **but have not found new ones that give us a sense of accomplishment with their passage.** Compounding this is the fact that many of us, perhaps most of us, do not recognize the worth of what we have, the value in what we have accomplished or how far we have come as people.

I can almost hear you saying, "Oh, no. Now Hillman's going to start running off on some sort of Zen trip, like 'Inner peace is worth more than gold, Grasshopper' (Grasshopper was Kane's name in the Kung Fu TV series). Well, Hillman, inner peace doesn't pay the rent."

Okay, you're right; inner peace doesn't pay the rent. But, since you have to pay the rent anyway, whether you're miserable or not, having some sort of inner peace couldn't hurt. In fact, it might even make you feel a bit better about having to pay the rent in the first place. Let's look at this another way.

Have you ever seen how someone who doesn't have kids reacts to the noise and general confusion other people's kids make? Have you ever noticed how he or she flinches and cringes at each and every bang, scream or crash made by other folks' kids, especially when the kids' parents don't seem to notice? What we have here is an example of two very different perspectives on the noise the kids are making. On one hand, the person without kids probably has a relatively peaceful life. At home, things are quiet, especially if the person is single. He or she can listen to the music of his or her choice without interruption, can watch the television programs he or she chooses the same way. He or she can sit down and read a good book, prepare and eat dinner, practice yoga or snuggle in front of the fireplace during an intimate evening with his or her significant other, all in the calm serenity of a childless home. Anything that upsets this atmosphere of tranquility, even if temporarily, is noticed and often resented.

The parent, on the other hand, has no atmosphere of tranquility. There are no peaceful meals; no uninterrupted books, music or television programs. And as for an intimate evening in front of the fireplace. . . .

For the parent, pandemonium is generally the rule, along with confusion, din, clutter, and chaos. How then, does the parent survive?

Well, in the first place, the parent learns to live with the noise. It gets tuned out to a large extent. Where the person not accustomed to the confusion finds it a distraction, the parent adapts by learning to concentrate in spite of it. In other words, the confusion, din, clutter, and chaos simply become part of the background and don't particularly matter.

But does this necessarily mean that the parent has no tranquility, no peace? And does it follow that the childless person, for all the serenity of his or her perfect, childless home, has more tranquility or peace?

Clearly the answer is **no**. Instead, for the busy, harried parent, the tranquility or peace come from sources other than living in a picture-perfect, Martha Stewart home. The single Yuppie and the parent are finding and measuring their peace according to different standards, by utilizing differing *currencies of gratification*.

What is a currency of gratification? Quite simply, it is anything that gives us pleasure.

A while ago we discussed currencies of approval at some length. We noted that as we grow, the rewards we seek in life—and the things that make us feel as though we have been rewarded—change. A first grader, for example, might be truly pleased if the good Sister Asthmatica draws a happy face on her test paper to signify that she did a good job on an assignment; but an adult would be mortified, angered, and chagrined if Mr. Stuffenbottom did no more than that to reward the successful acquisition of a major contract. The adult, in contrast to the child, wants a raise, a promotion or the key to the executive washroom. A happy face just doesn't make it.

If we understand that the currencies of approval in our life change, so too should we recognize that the currencies of gratification do and ought to change as well.

Let's return to our contrast between the childless Yuppie and the parent. The Yuppie would probably see nothing but clutter when viewing little Johnny's colorful scrawls hanging from magnets all over the refrigerator. The parent, however, sees progress, accomplishment, and a source of a certain pride in these same scrawlings. The Yuppie finds the collection of drawings messy; the parent sees them as a source of gratification.

Why is this important? To answer that, let's return to the questions we posed a few moments ago. Why, we asked, do so many supposedly normal, rational adults still feel unfulfilled, not-yet-accomplished, either somehow not yet really grown up, or, worse, as though they are missing out on something? How can we go through all the processes of individuation, through changing sources of approval, standards of approval and currencies of approval, through the differentiation between self and person and still not be—or at least not feel—complete? Why do so many people still feel that something is missing, even when they cannot define precisely what that something is?

I have suggested that at least one part of the answer is that too many of us have overlooked the process by which the currencies of approval in our lives change—or ought to change—as we grow and mature. Citing the famous Bruce Springstein song, we noted how many people long for the "Glory Days" of a past that can never be recaptured. Why do they feel this way? In large measure, I suggested, it was because they have not recognized that the currencies of approval that added the glory to those long-gone days are no longer appropriate to their current life. Hence, missing the familiar currencies of approval, they feel that most or all of the validation they once enjoyed is gone.

In similar fashion, those of us who have not progressed past the currencies of gratification of our younger, perhaps more carefree, days will undoubtedly find that as circumstances change the gratification we get out of life is diminished.

Let's take as an example a classic male chauvinist currency of gratification, the string of female conquests. Now, as misguided, misogynistic, and outdated as this might be in today's culture, the fact is that a vast majority of young men see such a string of conquests as both a currency of gratification and a currency of approval before their peers. In other words, beyond any sexual gratification they might get from their various involvements, the very fact of these multiple involvements is a source of gratification. Taking pleasure from the number of "trophies" they have amassed, they then parlay this into a means of gaining the approval of their peers as they show off or brag about their latest conquest. For them there is no value and stability in a long-term, committed relationship. They are too busy playing the field.

But this is a young man's game. So what happens

when Studly, having quite a number of conquests to his dubious credit over the years, reaches 40 and may even be at this point married? Does he find contentment in the life he has, or does he continue coming on to every woman he meets? Does he recognize his responsibilities, or does he play the dangerous game of flirt-and-see-what-happens, placing his home, family, reputation, peace of mind, and perhaps even his career in jeopardy? Does he age gracefully, or make a fool of himself by trying to attract young women half his age?

Does the term mid-life crisis come to mind?

Beyond this example, we needn't look far to find other perhaps less obvious situations where this dynamic comes into play.

What about the woman who willingly gives up her job to have a baby and then finds herself frustrated with the home-and-hearth daily grind that has taken the place of her power lunches and full schedule of important meetings? What about the couple who, deciding to have a family, find themselves resenting the fact that the adult vacations they once enjoyed have been replaced by trips to Disney World with several kids in tow? What of the couple who takes in one of their elderly, widowed parents, only to find they sorely miss the privacy they had before Mom or Dad moved in? What about the person who retires from a position only to discover that without the job life has lost a lot of its meaning?

Not everyone experiences problems such as these. There are quite a few people who do successfully make these and other transitions and find satisfaction in their new circumstances. In other words, they recognize and accept the new currencies of gratification in their lives and do not pine for the ones they have had to leave behind.

I have a good friend who lived the successful Yuppie life until he was 37. His house was impeccably furnished; his large wrap-around sectional couch alone cost almost $5,000. His books, CDs, and record albums were all shelved in perfect order; he had one closet for casual clothes and one for dress clothes. He had one drawer for light socks and one for dark socks. His kitchen was beautifully wallpapered, the chairs around his dining table tastefully upholstered in an elegant off white, his refrigerator was uncluttered, and every dish looked as though it had just been bought. His brand new car was washed every few days and was as immaculate inside as the day he drove it out of the showroom.

Then he got married.

Today, several years, three children, three cats, and a dog later, his couch has been shredded by the cats, his books are mostly in storage since he lost his den to a nursery. His clothes are all crammed into one closet; his socks are stuffed into an overfilled drawer with his underwear. His CDs and record albums are hopelessly out of order. There is Magic Marker ink on his wallpaper, his dining room chairs sport various stains from blueberry yogurt and tomato sauce, and his refrigerator is festooned with school notices and first-grade drawings, half his dishes are chipped and his way cool sports car has been long since replaced by the family van.

But, he is happier than I have ever seen him.

Was this an easy transition? No, it was not. But somehow, somewhere along the way, he learned that the wallpaper just wasn't all that important, that the pleasure, the gratification he gained from watching his baby daughter master the intricacies of a fork and spoon were worth a few stains on the dining chairs. He found that a long weekend spent camping with his sons and the

Scouts were worth the loss of a long weekend in Montreal with his wife. He found value in having the couch, tattered though it may be, filled with his kids and perhaps a few of their friends as they all watched a movie together.

Is my friend a saint? Is he a genius? No, he is decidedly neither (in fact, he can be a bit of an idiot). What he is, however, is fortunate in having successfully made the transition in both his currencies of approval and his currencies of gratification.

Now, that said, I repeat, **it is not easy**. Finding that you and your spouse can no longer easily escape to Florida for a long weekend because there is no one to watch the kids, finding that the money you might have once spent on clothes, jewelry or a fancy restaurant now must be earmarked for another use, finding that your privacy has been invaded, your social life shot and your sex life reduced to a random occurrence is not easy.

Adjusting to retirement is not easy. Making the transition from being a high-profile corporate employee with a corner office on the 47th floor to becoming a part-time consultant with an office in the basement is not easy.

Getting older, getting grayer, watching your body sag, and looking in the mirror and seeing your father or mother staring back at you is not easy.

But none of these situations are made any easier by pining for what once was, by missing what will never be again or by resenting what is.

And so, Grasshopper, while it is true that inner peace will never pay the rent, it can make paying the rent seem like a bit less of a burden.

❦ ❦ ❦

CHAPTER 18

Me and Bobby McGee

ta ta ta

"Freedom's just another word for nothing left to lose. . . ." So goes the old Kris Kristofferson song, and it holds a gem of truth. Many of us wish we could be free. But what does being free really mean? What does it entail?

For many, if not most people, being free means being in complete control, having to account to no one, answer to no one, being free to make one's own choices and, perhaps, one's own mistakes. It often means being free to do as we want, when we want.

But is this freedom that so many of us miss, this control so many of us long for, truly possible? Or is it in reality simply another way of looking at "**nothing left to lose**"?

To answer this question, I want to return to the concept of control we discussed earlier. You'll recall that in discussing this idea we mentioned self-control and touched upon the concept of our control over our daily lives. We discussed how control works, the difference between what we can and cannot control, recognizing the difference between the two, and developing a strategy for exerting the control we do have.

We examined the Cardless Card Trick and discussed the notion of facilitating our environment. We talked about effective control, and defined it as the ability to make someone else do something we want them to do . . . or, more to the point, the ability to make someone else do something they do not want to do, or normally would not want to do.

We discussed the three ways effective control works: through the use of aggression, through neurotic conflict or through the establishment of a sense of competence. We discussed parallel value tracks and the ways they can lead us to a sense of conflict. We discussed manipulation and how it is often used on us.

Now, I'd like to take another look at the issue of control and suggest that if you want to refresh the ideas we have already discussed concerning control you should take a quick glance at Chapter 7. Specifically, here I want to look at the issue of control through the prism of a concept we have just discussed, the notion of rites of passage and the ways in which they are, or are interpreted as being, milestones in our lives.

What is a milestone? It is a marker along a road or railroad track that lets travelers know how far they have come on their journey and how far they yet have to travel towards their destination. In other words, a milestone marks progress.

When we discussed rites of passage, we were essentially talking about the same thing. These rites were specifically intended (in the case of ancient religious or cultural tests of adulthood) or are interpreted today (as in graduation from high school, achieving the age of majority, sexual activity or getting one's own apartment) as marking our progress from childhood to adulthood. However, unlike the journey one might make on a hike, in a car or on a train or plane, the journey to adulthood does not have a specific endpoint as its destination.

Reaching adulthood, for one thing, can be defined in several ways: physically, socially, economically, chronologically, emotionally, legally or culturally. No one thing makes you an adult. Further, there is a difference between being considered an adult and having grown up or truly matured. With the benefit of hindsight, many of us can point to occasions when, even though we were considered adult by most popular measures, we still had growing up to do, growing up that might have taken still a few more years to complete.

Beyond this, we should recognize that there is no entry point to adulthood. You do not pass through a gate, cross a border or have your passport stamped upon arriving at adulthood. It is a **condition**, rather than a place or even a time.

Unfortunately, the message is lost on most of us as we travel the road from childhood through adolescence, our teenage years, and into our twenties, thirties, and beyond. Having lived a certain number of years, we think we are grown up. We think we have achieved something beyond mere age. We sense that, somehow, we should be in control of our lives in a way we never have been before.

And, usually, we are disappointed.

The question we have to ask, once again, is why?

We have essentially posed these questions before, if perhaps in a slightly different way:

- Why do so many of us still feel unfulfilled?
- Why do so many of us still feel controlled by others?

- Why do so many of us still feel as though we don't control our own lives?

I have suggested that at least one answer to the first question is the fact that many of us do not recognize the changing currencies of approval and currencies of gratification in our lives. Just as it is widely recognized that the patterns of interpersonal relations, socialization, family structure, and culture that we learn as children are largely imprinted upon us for life, it should be equally recognized that the currencies of approval and currencies of gratification to which we learn to respond when we are young also stay with us for years and years. Until we learn that as adults (however that status is defined) we must respond to new currencies of approval and currencies of gratification, we are all but doomed to experience the crisis, frustration or ego bruise known as **unfulfillment**.

But let's turn to the second and third questions posed a moment ago. Where is the freedom many of us expected to experience as we passed from pre-adulthood to adulthood? Why do so many of us still feel as though we don't control our own lives, feel that we are controlled by others?

The answer, as distasteful as it may be, is that many of us feel this way because in large measure we don't control our own lives and we are controlled by others.

Now, before you protest by tossing this book across the room, look at it this way: If you have a job, the Boss, your professional responsibilities, and even the corporate culture of your employer control your life to a very large extent. Unless you want to quit your job, you cannot take time off unless you have vacation days coming to you. You generally can't dress as you might want to, but rather have to dress as your professional situation dictates. Sitting there at your desk, working at the counter, or at your place on the sales floor, you can't take a nap in the middle of a dreary, rainy fall afternoon. You probably have to work more hours than you might want to, on days when you might not want to, and doing things beyond those you might find pleasant or gratifying. You have to acknowledge the hierarchy of your workplace, its no smoking rules, its 30-minute or 60-minute lunch break schedule, and its rules of conduct. In short, if you accept the job, you must also accept its explicit control over a large portion of your existence.

If you are married, you are similarly constrained. You can't go off with the attractive person who catches your eye on that business trip; you can't simply disappear for a weekend. You can't decide to paint the walls of your house black with no regard to your partner's opinion on the matter, and you probably can't announce that you are not going to waste your time by spending another holiday with your spouse's family ever again. In other words, if you accept the security of work or the comforts of marriage, you must also accept that you have given control over yet another large segment of your life to someone else.

If you have children, then you know how little of your own life you control. The children's welfare and needs have to come first. So, the fancy two-seat sports car gives way to the family van. The vacations to Hedonism II are replaced by the vacation at Disney World. The money otherwise spent on a new suit now goes toward tuition, dance lessons, your daughter's new sneakers, your son's new skateboard, and, in all probability, way too many Christmas presents. The deck of your dreams remains just that, a dream, while the money that might have made it a reality goes towards orthodontia. If you are a parent, the list goes on and on . . . and it all spells a loss of control over your own life, as you have to constantly make accommodations to the needs of the children. Your needs come second and your wants come in a distant third . . . if at all.

None of this even begins to speak to the control over your life represented by laws, social norms, and the need most of us feel to be accepted by others.

All these examples point to the fact that when we accept something into our lives—a job and its attendant paycheck and security, a spouse or relationship partner, or a child—we also give up something. Seen one way, what we give up is a measure of control over our lives and daily choices. Seen another way, what we give up is **freedom**. To make this point a bit more clear, think of your life as an empty closet. Now, you might revel in all the empty storage space in there, but you can't wear the empty space to work or on that big date next Saturday night. To be properly prepared for those occasions, you will need clothes. But where will these clothes be stored? Why, in the closet, naturally.

But, the moment you hang a suit or dress in the closet, you have given up something, namely, some of that empty storage space you were so happily reveling in earlier. In other words, and to borrow an analogy from physics, the value of the empty closet was potential; it only became kinetic when you actually began storing clothes there. In time, as you acquire more clothes, the available space in the closet will be further reduced until the closet eventually becomes full. Now, you have no storage space left, but you do have a closet full of clothes. The question is which has the greater value to you, the empty storage space or the clothes?

So it is with our lives. In a pure state of nature, our lives resemble the empty closet. They are free of encumbrances, duties, responsibilities, obligations, and the control of others. We are, in this state, free. But with every relationship we take on, whether a professional relationship in the form of a job or a personal relationship of one sort or another (marriage, children, friends, etc.), a bit of space in that empty closet is taken up. In time, our lives are full of encumbrances, duties, responsibilities, obligations, and at least some control by others over portions of our lives. The question again is which is of more value to us, the life free of encumbrances or the life complicated by the demands of others and our duties and obligations toward them?

Yet, many of us do not look at it this way. Rather, upon belatedly realizing that we have lost the control or freedom we thought we'd enjoy in life, many of us become frustrated; this, somehow, is not what we expected. But perhaps it is not the situation that is wrong, but rather the expectation that is ill-founded. Perhaps we should begin by recognizing that when we were children, parents, teachers, and others in authority exerted control over perhaps 95 percent of our lives, but as adults others still control 80 percent or more of our lives in one way or another. In other words, nothing has really changed, even though we thought it had—or should have—when we became adults.

Being an adult, however that status is defined, does not necessarily give us complete control over our lives. Further, it was never meant to. Unless we choose to live the life of a hermit like Thoreau, we are bound to make countless accommodations to the world around us. To mourn, decry or resent the absence of that control, therefore, is, as Mr. Spock would put it, **illogical**. It is a waste of our emotional and psychological energy that not only saps our strength, but also tends to blind us to the facts of what we can control. The trick is making the best choices we can regarding how we live, respond, and interact with others at home and at work.

Now, there is a way to regain all that freedom. We could quit our jobs and abandon our spouses or partners and kids. We could, like Thoreau, live alone in the woods, turn our backs on human companionship (not to mention indoor plumbing!), refuse to pay our taxes and take our chances.

Thus stripped bare of human encumbrances, we truly would be free, but such freedom would also be the **"nothing left to lose"** that Kristofferson sings about.

The solution, I suggest, is not to resent the lack of freedom in our lives, but rather to recognize the new currencies of approval and gratification inherent in these circumstances, relationships, and responsibilities.

To sum up, I suggest that much of the disconnection we feel between the way things are and the way we sensed they would be or ought to be comes from three basic mistakes many of us make as adults:

- We fail to take into account the changing currencies of approval and currencies of gratification operating in our lives as time passes. We miss the status, achievements, and perhaps pleasures and freedoms we might once have enjoyed (or hoped to enjoy) and also fail to see the value of what we have and where we are.

- We mistake the rites of passage in our lives, the milestones, and the status and rights we thought they gave us, for real progress. In other words, like the Cowardly Lion, we look to external testimonials—in his case, a medal for bravery; in our case, perhaps graduation, an apartment, a real job, marriage, and the birth of our first child—for the validation we expect as adults. We are, many of us, grown-ups without having, in many cases, actually, grown up.

- We make the crucial mistake of believing that our status as adults will grant us freedom from the control or influence of others . . . and then resent the fact that so much of the control we thought we would be exercising is an illusion.

Complete freedom is, it turns out, nothing left to lose. For everything in our lives, every relationship, support, emotional or financial comfort that we would not want to lose, there is a cost. That cost is a bit of freedom and a bit of absolute control over our own lives. We are so accustomed, as a consumer society, to the concept of buying things that we never question the notion of cost when it comes to material possessions. We want that fur, that ring, that new car or other toy. To obtain these things, we pay the necessary cost. Perhaps we should also recognize that there are also costs to the web of relationships, personal and professional, that define our lives. Why, we might ask ourselves, should we not recognize that these too have a price, a cost associated with them? More to the point, why should we **resent** paying this price any more than we would resent paying for the fur, the ring or the car?

Now, this is not to say that any price at all is acceptable. The price of living with an abusive spouse, for example, is too high no matter what one might think one gets out of a relationship. The price of working for an abusive boss or in a job that demands far more than it gives back can also be too high. These are choices we have to make just as we might decide that a car, house or any other item costs more than we are willing or able to pay. Each given circumstance or relationship requires us to decide whether the cost is worth the reward. But the important thing to recognize here is that **there is a cost** to every relationship, professional or personal. That prior recognition alone, I suggest, can go a long way toward addressing and answering the issue of why we might not have the freedom or enjoy the control we once thought we might expect to enjoy. At minimum, it is something to think about.

CHAPTER 19

See Spot Run

≥≥ ≥≥ ≥≥

When it comes to almost any human activity, there are generally three kinds of people. There are **under-achievers**, **overachievers**, and the rest of us in the vast, **broad middle**. And so it is with work, although we can identify several more subsets within these three expansive categories when we think about work and the ways people approach it.

There are people who work because they have to, and those who don't even though they should. There are those who work to get ahead and those who work to get by. There are those who do the least they can get away with, those who do what they have to, and those who always do their best. Finally, in a rarefied place few of us ever visit for long, there are those who consistently go above and beyond the normal call of duty, those who always hit the home run no matter what. These are the **overachievers** and within the context of this book, we should pause a moment and take a look at these people and consider what makes them tick. Why?

There are three reasons. **The first** is that overachievers are often held up to the rest of us as models of what we ought to be. It is not uncommon within many working environments for various awards to be given out to recognize the Employee/Salesperson/Manager of the Month/Year. You can read small squibs about these people in the People or Community section of your local newspaper, read about them in almost any corporate newsletter in the country, and even see their photographs posted in your neighborhood supermarket. It is clear that while management wants to recognize and reward these people for their achievement, they also want to motivate the rest of us to copy the example of these hard-working folks and give our all to our jobs.

Similarly, when promotions are handed out at most firms, the work ethic and performance of those being promoted are usually headlined as an example for the rest of us, the message being, "See, work hard like Smith, here, and you too might be promoted." So the first reason to look at overachievers is that they are **held up** as examples.

The **second reason** for examining overachievers is the impact or effect they have on those around them, whether family, co-workers or simply fellow employees. On occasion, overachievers make those around them happy; but on the other hand they very frequently make everyone around them completely miserable.

Finally, **the third** reason for examining overachievers is that they are not always the happy people most of us assume them to be. And since there might be an overachiever or two among my readers, I think it might be important for them to have a word or two said about the situation in which they find themselves.

But let's begin by asking a simple question: What is an **overachiever**? By the very term we understand that it is someone who not only achieves a goal, but also does so in a way, to a degree and with a consistency that most people do not. So it is not the guy who makes that big sale who is the overachiever. Rather, it is the guy who makes big sales all the time, the one who steals the competition's biggest account, and at the same time opens a market no one else could get a foot into.

It is not the woman who sells the most expensive house that the agency has listed who is the overachiever. But rather it is the woman who makes that sale when everyone else on the staff knew the place was over priced and had essentially given up. It is the woman who sold the place when four other agencies had been unable to move it after more than a year of trying. She is the woman who, simultaneously, moved three other impossible properties. It is not the person who stays late at work to finish a project or presentation who is the overachiever. Rather, it is the person who stays late every night and who works every weekend, on both Saturday and Sunday. And so it is not any one thing that makes the overachiever, but rather it is a **pattern**. For this reason, we can take luck out of the equation, because, due to luck, almost anyone can make that startlingly big sale once in a while. Being in the right place at the right time, or just happening across the right buyer can produce the sale that everyone else envies or thought was impossible. But luck rarely strikes twice and luck never strikes consistently, week after week, month after month or year after year. Success on that scale usually takes skill and hard work, work so hard, in fact, that most of us don't try to put forth that sort of effort on anything approaching a regular basis.

A friend of mine tells a story about one such person, someone he knew years ago while in grad school.

My friend had a part-time job in the local branch of a very well known, up-scale, national department store. He worked in the ladies' shoe department. When he first took the position, everyone in the department was on a straight salary, just like all the store's other employees. Then the corporate headquarters decided upon an experiment: they would put the chain's five most highly producing shoe departments on a 10% commission and see what happened. As my friend tells the story, this one guy quickly emerged as a classic "overachiever." It began with the fellow shaving, first ten, then fifteen, then thirty minutes off his lunch hour so as to not miss time on the sales floor. He came in when he was visibly sick, so as to not miss potential sales. Finally taking a vacation, he called every day to ask what new merchandise had come in and then cut his vacation short when he learned that a shipment of expensive, imported Italian shoes had come in. During a particularly severe blizzard, during which the governor declared a State of Emergency and ordered all businesses in the area closed, this fellow tromped to work anyway and stood there pounding on the door, demanding of the empty building that he be let in. While my friend to this day dismisses this fellow as, "a nut," I see in the example an overachiever who lost perspective . . . as very many of them do.

Now this is not to say that in some cases of apparent overachievement, other factors are at work as well. One such factor, for example, is the so-called fast track.

It is not at all uncommon for certain people in larger corporate settings to be placed on something called the fast track, that is, a series of postings and promotions that are specifically designed and timed to bring that person along to a position of high corporate responsibility in a relatively short time. But, as anyone who knows a fast-tracked person can tell you, the sacrifice that usually goes along with the fast track would make most people think twice, if not shudder. The fast-tracked person may find himself posted to a foreign country where he really has no desire to be. The fast-tracked person may find herself relocated to different states or regions of the country three times in four years. Home becomes wherever he or she happens to be at the moment. Many of the things that the rest of us take for granted, a stable personal life, personal relationships, acquiring things for our homes, holidays with friends and family, often become mere memories for the fast-tracked person. Moreover, in place of these traditional comforts, this person usually has an inordinate amount of work to fill in the time you or I might spend with friends and loved ones. And, since personal relationships are often one prime casualty of the fast-track career, when they are not working, a lot of fast trackers are lonely. So to say that a person was promoted because of a fast-track, without recognizing the personal sacrifices that go into that life, is to ignore the actual consistent pattern of that life. Essentially, the fast-tracked person is an overachiever whose only difference is that he or she is doing this overachieving in a variety of places, rather than just in the office.

But right about now I can hear someone saying, "Yeah, but Mark, what about favoritism? A lot of people get promoted because they're the Boss' nephew or worse, because they're sleeping with the boss. It's infuriating. Now you mean to tell me that these people are overachievers?"

No. I am not trying to say that everyone who gets anything is an overachiever. Yes, there are, unfortunately, people who get ahead because of something that someone else gives them, for whatever reason. But by definition, if they received something because someone else gave it to them, then they have not achieved it; they have not accomplished it on their own. They therefore cannot, by definition, be overachievers. So, along with luck, we can cross favoritism off our list of reasons for why over-achievers accomplish the things they do. But we should also remember that the well-known Peter Principle[1] very often, if not usually, comes in to eventually derail the success of the person who rises through favoritism. Sooner or later, if this person truly lacks the talent to handle the task at hand, even favoritism will not be able to advance him or her much further.

So, no matter which way you cut it, slice it or dice it, overachievers get probably 80% of what they accomplish through sacrifice and hard work.

"Yeah?" you might ask, "what's the other 20%?"

Well, the other 20% is probably made up of a combination of things. It just might be that at least some of these people really are more talented or smarter than the rest of us. It might be that they have a proclivity for schoolwork, for sales, for management, foreign policy, human relations or a host of other things. It might not hurt if the overachiever is, in addition to being smarter or more talented, also unusually attractive. Numerous studies have shown that for both men and women there is a definite and measurable advantage to being more attractive than average.[2] It is a fact that good-looking people are not only preferred for dates, friendships and jobs, they're also believed to have more intelligence and integrity.[3] And as if this weren't enough, they are usually the first ones noticed in any setting. Thus, being attractive gives the overachiever even more advantage. Then there is also the sheer notice that comes from just being an overachiever.

The overachiever is likely to be touted by the Boss, shown off to colleagues, and introduced at company conferences. All this leads to, again, being noticed and that typically results in even more opportunities. So, yes, we can say that maybe 20% of what the overachiever achieves doesn't come directly from hard work, but about 80% does. What does that say to the rest of us? Are we failures because we don't overachieve? Should we really feel badly about ourselves and prod ourselves to greater lengths in an effort to match the accomplishments of the overachiever? Probably not.

The comparison between the average person and the overachiever is more complex than it might at first blush appear; truth in this case is multi-layered. The overachiever, for example, often sacrifices personal relationships in the drive to do and achieve even more. While some are well adjusted, well-rounded people, many are not. The overachiever may find himself cut off from family, with few real friends. The overachiever may find her marriage crumbling, her family, even her children, if she has any, estranged. Community involvement for many overachievers is simply nonexistent, so a sense of belonging, connecting them to something larger than themselves (other than the organization for which they work) is often lacking from their lives. All of these things must be compared to the life of the average person for the equation to be at all valid. True, a certain person may not volunteer for extra hours at work, may not come in on weekends, and may not take work home every night. But that same person may be a loving and involved parent, an adult leader for the Boy Scouts, the Little League or the girls' soccer team. That person may be active in his or her religious congregation, or volunteer at a local food pantry on a regular basis. The work-oriented overachiever rarely has time for all these things. And so the question must be asked, in terms other than business and career, is the overachiever actually a success as a person?

Now, before anyone accuses me of being the champion of mediocrity, let me remind you of our earlier discussion of parallel value tracks. In that discussion we established that we all have these parallel value tracks that act as our behavioral guides for the different and separated portions of our lives. We discussed how a person might have a work value track, a family value track, one for close friends, and one for acquaintances. Within each of these value tracks exists a set of standards by which we assess what is expected of us in a given situation or relationship, what we can expect from that situation or relationship, and how we ought to act within that situation or relationship. This much we recognize.

But we also touched upon what happens when two or more of these value tracks collide, as when the Boss wants you to make that big presentation the same morning Mama wants you to take her to see her podiatrist, the amazing Dr. Bunion. This issue of colliding value tracks, however, brings us to something that we may not at first recognize, namely that there also exists within each of us an overarching value track into which all the others fit. It is this overarching value track that informs us of the relative importance of the other varied everyday value tracks in our lives; it helps us keep straight which of these are the most important, which are of lesser importance, and which are the least important. The conflict we experience when Mama and the Boss both expect something from us at the same time comes from the fact that our overarching value tracks tell us that both are important. In this case, the overarching value track may ultimately tell us that Mama and Dr. Bunion will just have to wait, that work and the Boss come first. But, it is also possible that the message we might get is that Mama comes first and the Boss will have to find someone else to make that big presentation. This calculation is often the difference between the overachiever and the rest of us, and it is here that we find the answer for those who might accuse us of being satisfied with mediocrity if we don't strive to overachieve.

For it could be that in our personal calculus, Mama, our kids, the Little League, a stable family life, our hobbies, our congregation or whatever are more important than work is and, ultimately, more important than the rewards work has to offer.

I have a friend who is doing OK financially, not great, better than most, but not nearly as well as he could be doing. I once asked him why he doesn't work more and make more money. "Simple," he said, "I just don't want to work that hard." He went on to explain that by working only four to six hours most days (and from home, at that!), he is free to look after his young daughter, free to be involved in the lives of his teen-aged sons, and free to do a good deal of what needs doing around the house so his wife doesn't have to do it all when she comes home from her job at a major corporation. My friend has made a calculation that the time with his kids is more important than a new car, more important than a new DVD player and, in the end, more important than what his W-2 says.

But to the overachiever this calculation rarely needs to be made, because work always comes first. It comes before family; it comes before vacation. It comes before Saturdays at the Little League ball field, outings with the Scouts or afternoons coaching the girls' basketball team. It comes before dinners at home, and it comes

before the holiday gatherings which most of us look forward to. In the hit movie Cast Away, Tom Hanks plays
just this sort of overachiever. In a scene that comes just
before the incident that sets up the bulk of the story,
Hanks' character is sitting with friends and loved ones at
Christmas dinner when his beeper goes off. Without a
word of complaint he gets up from the table and, after
calling the office, prepares to leave for the Pacific coast of
Siberia. Now, most of us would never do such a thing.
Most of us would resent having our holiday meal inter-
rupted by a call from the office. Most of us, in fact, would
not be wearing the damned beeper on Christmas to begin
with. But for the overachiever, work and/or its varied
(and often questionable) rewards are more important
than just about everything.

The overachiever does wear his beeper to the holiday dinner table. The overachiever does leave her cell
phone on during a wedding. The overachiever does
bring the laptop and a pile of work on the family vacation, if he even actually goes. The overachiever makes
calculations that most of us would think absurd. If you
had booked a vacation cruise with a non-refundable price
of $1,200 a person, wouldn't you feel that you should go?
Would you not look at, among other things, the $1,200
you invested, $1,200 you cannot get back? Most of us
would. Yet the overachiever often sees things differently.
I know of at least one overachiever who, after booking
just such a family vacation ($1,200 x 4!) bailed out on the
morning of the family's departure because he "just could
not get away from work." The lost $1,200 did not even
phase him. Again, his overarching value track told him
that down time with his family, a chance to rekindle the
relationship with his wife, time to bond with his teen-
aged sons and the $1,200 he was going to lose on his tick-

et, were all less important than being at his desk.

A bit later in this discussion we will examine the rewards for which the overachiever works and take a look at the calculations and rationalizations he or she often makes. For now, however, it is essential just to realize that the overarching value track that most of us use to rank the individual value tracks in our segmented lives are not really necessary for the overachiever: his or her decision is already made. But that does not diminish the value of what the rest of us decide is most important in our lives. Far from being satisfied with mediocrity, it is usually the case that those of us who do not strive to overachieve have simply found other things, other value tracks that are more important, more satisfying or more urgent than the demands of work and its associated value track.

Now, that said, this is not an excuse for refusing to hold down a job. This is not an excuse for sitting in front of the TV all day, eating bon-bons, slurping beer, and watching Jerry Springer. It is not a free pass for laziness. What it is, however, is recognition that those of us who are not overachievers in work or career may nonetheless be significant achievers in other areas. But if this is true, why do so many of us have a truly negative reaction to overachievers?

WHEN YOU THINK YOU DON'T MEASURE UP, IT'S OFTEN TIME TO GET A DIFFERENT YARDSTICK!

Before we answer this question, however, it is important to differentiate between the overachievers we may encounter in our lives. Few of us seem to mind the overachiever who happens to be a sports star. Rather, we admire the likes of Mickey Mantle, Venus Williams, Joe Namath, Michael Jordan or Tiger Woods. Even though hard work goes into the perfection of their art, most of us recognize that they are displaying a rare God-given talent and even people who are not particularly sports fans acknowledge the rare gift these people possess. Similarly, while musical tastes differ widely, few people actually resent the success of a Pavarotti, a Garth Brooks or a Sinatra (opinions concerning Britney Spears not with-standing!). Few people resent the accomplishments of a Donald Trump, a Henry Kissinger or a Bill Gates, yet they are all overachievers by almost any standard. So why is it that we acknowledge, even applaud, the achievements of these people (again, with the exception of Britney Spears!), and yet resent or feel uncomfortable with the accomplishments of certain other overachievers? At least one reason, I would suggest, is the degree of **immediacy** these famous people just mentioned have to our lives. A perfect example of this can be found as close as your television.

Few of us, watching Katie Couric or any of a host of other TV personalities resent their success. Most of us have never even thought about where these people came from. We don't know their career paths, how they got where they are or what that one big break might have been that catapulted them to national exposure. We simply accept them as the faces and voices we see on the TV news. But the truth is that all of these people started somewhere. All of them started out as a nobody before he or she became a somebody. And all of them left other people, usually co-workers, but sometimes friends, behind.

Within the past few years an example of this occurred in my hometown. A certain unheralded local

TV news anchor happened to be noticed by the president of her network as he tuned in the local affiliate station while on a quiet, private vacation in our area. He was impressed with what he saw and within 48 hours this particular reporter was whisked to New York City, had changed her last name, and was made part of the national team. People around the country who did not know her merely saw her as a new face. But those she left behind, both on her own station and those of her competitors may have felt a different way. They may have resented the success, the sudden overachiever status. What's the difference between these people and the millions of others around the country who now see her face on TV and think nothing of it?

The difference is the **immediacy** she had in the lives of those who know her, as opposed to the millions who don't. You and I never competed against this woman. You and I never worked with her, saw her faults. You or I never had to stack our work up against hers. Similarly, you and I never sang in a competition against Pavarotti. We never competed against Tiger Woods or Mark McGuire, while waiting for our big break. So their success never diminished us. It took place outside of our personal world.

But the overachiever in our office, in our class or on our team is a different story. Here, the competition, even if unspoken, is immediate. Here, the prizes and rewards are finite. If Garth Brooks wins a Grammy Award, we are not diminished because we, in all probability, were not nominated for that award. McGuire's 70th home run did not come at our expense. But when the office overachiever wins that promotion, we can and do feel some loss. We realize that we can no longer win the prize he or she won. And, being human, we often resent it. We resent people we knew in the trenches, people we knew when they and we were nobodies, suddenly whisked into the rarefied air of the upper echelon. As we sit in our cramped cubicles, doing the same drudgework we've done for years, we resent the overachiever's spacious new office. We resent seeing him or her greeting important clients and watching the door close in our faces as they have important meetings with the top brass. And sometimes we actually get depressed over all this. Why, we sometimes wonder, do we never seem to get the big breaks? Why can't we succeed like that? Many of us ask, "What's wrong with me?"

The answer is that, in most cases, **nothing is wrong with us**; and this is an important lesson to learn when faced with an overachiever in our midst.

We have devoted a good portion of this book discussing things we seek or pursue in our lives. We have discussed several ways of making ourselves crazy, from chasing operating fantasies to trying to exert control over things completely beyond our influence. Well, here's another one: **comparing our lot in life to that of another person**, especially that of an overachiever, is a sure-fire short cut to being miserable. There's an old saying that goes "I cried because I had no shoes, until I saw a man who had no legs." The message is that, when comparing lives and fortunes, most of us naturally look up at those who have what we do not. People who do this very often feel cheated. Unfortunately rare is the person who looks down at those who have less and feels blessed.

Two recent news stories that ran at almost the same time provide a prime example of this. A West Coast man recently came forward as the winner of a rare super lottery jackpot, something in the neighborhood of $100 million. All across the country, people probably read that story and felt a twinge of jealousy. Yet, at just about the same time, there was another story about a young man who was struck by lightening on a beach in Massachusetts. There wasn't a cloud in the sky when this young man, tossing a football with some friends, was hit by a bolt discharged from a storm a few miles off shore. In both cases, the odds against the event were astronomical. Both were, literally, freak events, against all probability and entirely impossible to predict. Yet I wonder how many people envying the twist of fate that landed the man in California $100 million paused to consider the equally random twist of fate that killed the boy in Massachusetts.

Feeling diminished by the accomplishments of an overachiever, I think, is similar to wishing that random luck would reward us with a lottery jackpot without admitting that random luck can also kill us, for in both cases we are looking at only one side of the equation. **Focusing on what we don't have usually blinds us to what we do have.** Looking at what others have, similarly, leaves us disregarding what we have.

As an illustration of this, I'll use the example of a woman I know. In her thirties this woman found herself unemployed with no real training, no particular career path, and few attractive options. The victim of a string of bad-choice relationships, she was single and living with het mother with no suitors in sight. A serious gynecological problem brought her within a hair's breadth of a hysterectomy. And then she was diagnosed with cancer. Things were unquestionably bleak.

Yet within a few years she had beaten the cancer and was in complete remission. Volunteer work on a campaign while she'd been unemployed brought her to the attention of a prominent elected official who hired her for a position she'd never even dreamed of seeking. She met a wonderful man and got married at the age of 38. They bought a lovely home, and at 41, in spite of a reoccurrence of the gynecological problem and a tough pregnancy, she gave birth to a beautiful, healthy baby boy. One would think that she would count her blessings.

Instead, she envies the friend who married an overachiever who makes big money and inherited a house in a nearby neighborhood. This, in spite of the fact that the friend's husband leaves for work at 5 in the morning, doesn't return until 9 at night, sleeps in a separate bedroom, has no relationship with his wife or kids, and is on a fast track to a heart attack because of the stress related to his job. She envies the careers of those acquaintances whose jobs entail frequent travel, even though her son would make such travel problematic at best. She envies friends who have money to go on vacations, even though she and her husband bought a luxury car and own a boat. In short, this woman is making herself miserable by constantly looking at people who have things she doesn't have, all the while ignoring the truly amazing things she has herself.

And so it is with many of us when we look at the rewards accruing to the overachiever. We see the rewards, but not their cost. We see things we probably don't have, and ignore the things we do have. We envy the man with the fancier shoes, and ignore the man who has no legs.

But envy or a feeling of low comparative worth are not the only facets of living in the shadow of the overachiever. While most of us view the overachiever from a distance—even if that distance is just down the hall—those living closer to the overachiever, the husband or the kids, often experience an entirely different set of emotions; and that is what I want to discuss next.

The wife of one overachiever recently confided, "He thinks I want all this. He says that he's working 7 days a week, and even on holidays, for me and for the kids. But I was raised in the projects. I would have been happy in a bungalow or in a trailer park if I had a stable, loving relationship and a good home for my children. Instead I have this big house that's empty. I have two tables where no one ever sits for a meal. I have a huge, beautifully furnished bedroom where I sleep alone and where the intimacy of a husband and wife never occurs. I have children who are growing up spoiled and with a sense of entitlement because he throws things at them as a substitute for a relationship. I'm married, but I have 3 children growing up with no father. He came from a large family, but he's systematically cut off his relationships with his brothers and sisters. If they think of him at all, they think of him as a source of money and loans when they need them. He has no friends. I wanted to give him a party for his birthday and couldn't think of a single person to invite, except for people he works with. We've lived in three different states in 5 years. He never got to know anyone in the last neighborhood and now he doesn't know anyone here either. He has no time for anything but work. No time for me, no time for the kids, no time for anything."

Another spouse of an overachiever put the situation this way: "I didn't get married to be a single parent, but that's what I've become. When she got this promotion it wasn't a week before she started calling to say she'd be coming home late. Within a week, as I was making dinner, she began calling to say that she had a business dinner with this client or that one. She brings work home, goes in on weekends, and drags her laptop wherever we go so she can log on, check her e-mail, and 'squeeze in some work.' She missed our daughter's first day of school because she was halfway across the country for a week on business, and I've lost count of the nights I've fallen asleep as she sits in bed next to me, tapping away at her laptop until after midnight. It's becoming an **obsession** with her."

Another person added, "We had a cruise booked. At the last minute he said he couldn't go and I should go alone. I was mad as hell, but I went. I met a man on that cruise who seemed very interested, and I have to admit for a minute I thought, 'Why not? What do I have to lose?'"

Finally, the son of an overachiever said, "It's really weird. On the one hand he boasts about how not one person in 100 is like him, how no one has his drive. But at the same time, he expects me to be just like him. And when I'm not, he tells me I'm a failure, that I'll never cut it, that I'll never succeed like he did. But the point is, **I don't want to.**"

These few small, sad tales tell a wealth about what it can be like living with an overachiever, but before we go on, there is a clarification I want to make. A number of people reading this chapter might wonder why I am referring to overachievers, rather than workaholics, a term with which many people are familiar. Certainly, some readers might think, I have been describing the profile of what many people would consider to be a workaholic. But I have deliberately avoided that term because it is, although popular, not precise. To begin with, the term takes its obvious derivation from the word alcoholic. The alcoholic, we recognize, suffers from a disease. He or she is truly addicted to alcohol; it is a chemical, physical, as well as psychological dependency. The so-called workaholic, however, is rarely addicted to work . . . at least not in the physical sense. Rather, I view this person as an overachiever out of control, someone whose obsession with work may mask other psychological or emotional problems. While treatment of this person may require some decompression, it will never require the detoxification that a chemical dependency may require. I therefore feel that the word workaholic does a disservice to both the out-of-control overachiever and to the person suffering from a true chemical dependency.

Beyond this, the overachiever can come in many guises. Focused here on the work environment, we are viewing but one manifestation of overachievement. Chronic overachievement is a form of **compulsion**. Not the sort of compulsive behavior associated with someone who, say, can't stop washing her hands, but rather a compulsive perspective on aspects of everyday life. The dieter who becomes compulsive about weight loss and slips into anorexia and the runner or body builder who becomes compulsive and pushes his or her body beyond the extremes of physical endurance are overachievers. The so-called perfect mother may be an overachiever. The student who feels pressured to be number 1 in his class and cuts off all other activity in favor of grueling study is an overachiever. The super volunteer can be an overachiever. In short, anyone who allows one particular value track to overtake and dominate his or her life is an overachiever and is probably being compulsive to one degree or another.

Literature on eating disorders, to again use that example, has demonstrated that the compulsive dieter is not born that way and does not set out to develop an eating disorder. Rather, what may begin as a simple diet can grow out of proportion to the point where the person actually feels guilty about having eaten. She then slips into a stage where she either begins purging or literally starving herself in order to avoid the guilt associated with eating.

You may recall that in the opening paragraphs of this chapter I said the overachiever is characterized not by one accomplishment or action, but by a **pattern** of behaviors and accomplishments, always pushed to top the last achievement, always pushed to do more. So just as losing 20 pounds becomes not enough for the over-achieving dieter, just as cutting 10 seconds off his time in the 5 K race is not enough for the obsessed runner, being promoted becomes not enough for the overachiever in the work place. Just as there are always another 2 pounds to lose, just as there may always be another second shaved off the running time, for the overachiever in the work place there is always another promotion or another job to be won. But just as the anorexic's motivations for losing weight have gone out of control and often mask some deeper problem, the person who chronically strives to overachieve at work may have begun with laudable moti-vations and may be also masking some deeper issues through his or her overachieving actions.

One tragedy for the anorexics, or the body-builders who begin using steroids, is that they are destroying the very bodies they seek to perfect. So, too, the overachiever often winds up destroying the life he or she initially set out to build.

I have identified three types of workplace over-achievers. **The first** is the Hollywood/paperback ver-sion, those who knew in fourth grade that they were going to attend Harvard, graduate at the top of the class, and get a world-class job right out of the chute, let nothing stop them or distract them, accumulating their first million dollars before hitting age 25. Yeah, there are those people out there, but most of us are unlikely to meet many of them, no less find ourselves living with them. These are an extremely rare few and I frankly don't know whether to congratulate them on their vision and determination or dismiss them as a lunatic fringe. Either way, my interest is not with these superfolks, but rather with the other two categories I have identified: those who find themselves literally **seduced** into overachievement, and those who use the demands of overachievement as a way to **hide from or avoid** other issues or situations in life. Further, my interest in these people stems from the fact that they are much more likely to be the ones you or I are likely to find ourselves working with, married to or living with.

When patients come to my office because they are having difficulty living with the overachiever in their lives, they are much more likely to say that the overachiever's behavior began at a certain point in time, than they are to tell me that the person was like this before they met. My interest in these patients developed because they truly no longer recognize the overachiever as the person they were attracted to years ago.

You'll remember that in an earlier section of this book, I wrote about the "formal," early stages of relationships, when Your Nice meets His or Her Nice. As relationships develop, I wrote, the Nice is usually shed, dropped in favor of the informal person the Nice was masking. Faced with this informal person, the slob, the scatterbrained, the self-indulgent, many people come to me and ask "Where's the person I married, and how can I get this self-indulgent, sloppy, scatterbrained, impostor out of my house?" As you read, I usually explain to these patients that the self-indulgent, sloppy, scatterbrained, character is not an impostor at all; rather it really is the person he/she married, but when they met, the NICE was masking these charming traits under a heavy façade of formal behavior.

But with the person coming to me because the stranger living in their house is an overachiever, I truly think different dynamics are at work. For while the sloppy, scatterbrained or self-indulgent suitor can (and does) often hide these characteristics under a blanket of acceptable, even attractive formal behavior, the overachiever can rarely hide his/her drive. Indeed, most overachievers would not want to or would never think of doing so. More to the point, the established, practicing overachiever rarely has time for relationships, so it is fairly infrequent that a potential victim gets far enough into a relationship with one of these people to find him/herself deep into a troubled relationship. More often than not, the "relationship" dissolves long before it gets too serious, when the other person realizes that he/she does not want to sign onto some sort of permanent second-rate status, trailing behind the overachiever's career.

Rather, the example I run across far more frequently is the person, man or woman, who becomes involved with what they think is an average person, only to find 2, 5, or 10 years down the road that they are sharing little more than a mailbox with an overachieving absentee spouse. It is to these people that my heart goes out and it is for these people that I began to take a close look at the reasons behind the overachiever's behavior.

As I have said, I have defined three types of overachiever: the **born-to-it** Wunderkind, the "**seduced**" overachiever and those using their "**dedication**" to hide from some other issue.

Let us examine the victim of seduction first.

What does it mean to be "**seduced**?" The dictionary tells us that to seduce is, "to tempt, to lead astray, to entice into wrong." So, one who has been "seduced" has been tempted and, succumbing to that temptation, has been led astray. Seduction does not imply coercion or abduction; no one is, ultimately, "seduced" against their will; against his or her initial better judgment, perhaps, but not, in the end, against his or her will. Rather, the will of the seducer becomes the will of the seduced; seduction implies "surrender." Resistance becomes, in stages, bothersome, difficult, frustrating, and, in the end, seen as self-denying. The impulse to resist itself becomes resented, as the seducer wants it to be. The goals of the seducer are accepted and adopted by the one being seduced.

Similarly, seduction has a sense of almost languid time about it. It isn't hurried or rushed; the seduced person isn't making a snap decision here. He or she is enticed, bit-by-bit. The image, of tendrils slowly wrapping themselves about the victim until no escape is possible, comes to mind with the word seduction. Seduction is gradual; it isn't overwhelming. It doesn't announce itself; it doesn't frighten its prey into bolting. It doesn't give warning or often make its full intentions or cost clear.

Finally, as the temptation grows stronger, as the seduction works its course, not only are the victim's own doubts and misgivings stifled or ignored, but so are the warnings of friends and loved ones who see, as the victim cannot, the danger that lies just ahead. In the end, the seducer's voice is the only one the victim hears . . . or wants to hear.

What then do we make of the "seduced" over-achiever?

I use this term, **the seduced overachiever**, for two reasons. The first is to differentiate between this person and the man or woman who more properly fits into what I have already termed the "Hollywood/ paperback" over-achiever, the one who seems to know in fourth grade precisely what he or she wants out of life and how to get it. These people are the stuff of novels and movies. They are, to put it simply, born to their overachieving roles.

But the seduced overachiever rarely ever sets out to be an overachiever or pay the overachiever's price. Rather, most of these people started out much as you and I did. They stumbled here and bumbled there. They might have been intelligent; they might have had a good work ethic. But there was nothing that made them stand out. And then something happened.

This is the **second** reason why I use the term, **seduced** overachiever, because the "something" that happened usually entails a change in that person's actions and attitudes. And the changes do not come overnight. Extremely rare is the person who goes from being a caring, involved spouse or parent to an absentee within days. Rare also is the person who at first does not, at least tacitly, acknowledge the out-of-the-ordinary demands he or she is now beginning to accept and meet. But with time, this recognition and tacit admission stops. With time, the person changes and no longer necessarily sees the demands as being out of the ordinary or burdensome. With time, the person's focus changes. With time, he or she is seduced.

More often than not, the "something" that happens to start all this comes in the form of a promotion or new job. Sometimes it is a new business that the person started. Either way, accurately recognizing that the new job, position or business will require more effort than might have been the case in earlier endeavors, the person knuckles under and shoulders the task. At first, the out-of-the-ordinary demands, be they long nights, dinner meetings, business trips away from home, work brought home, or popping into the office on days off, are accepted as part of the territory and really no big deal. "It's only this once," "It's only this time of year," "It's only until we get through this project," are commonly heard rationalizations.

But the seduction continues. Perhaps there are certain perks. Maybe it is the opportunity to go on that business trip to London. It might be a conference in beautiful San Francisco. Maybe there's a bonus in the offing, or the chance to wield real power. Almost always, there is praise, either from superiors or fawning underlings. The head begins to get turned. Priorities shift. Soon, the rationalizations stop. There is, after all, no need for excuses or apologies for doing one's job, right? Why don't you/the kids/my parents/my so-called friends, just shut up and stop complaining that I'm not available for (fill in the blank)? Don't you all see that I'm on the way up here? Look at the money I'm making. Look at what I've been able to buy. Don't you want me to be a success? If you're going to just continually try to stand in my way, then maybe my life would be better without you. You, be a loser if you want. In fact, go find yourself another loser, if you want; I'm sure you'll be happy together wasting your time on (fill in the blank). But not me. **Me**, I'm a winner!

And so it goes . . . seduction complete.

An often-heard variation of this theme is, "I'm doing this for **you** or **you and the kids**." But this rings hollow as the spouse/children/family and friends of the overachiever begin to resent being abandoned, as the material rewards pale in comparison to the attention they really want and as it becomes clear that the overachiever is actually getting more out of the situation than those he/she suggests are the real beneficiaries.

How does this happen; why does it happen?

I believe that there are three possible dynamics here, sometimes working separately, sometimes working in tandem. The first is the **affirmation dynamic**, often mistaken for greed or materialism.

Under the influence of the affirmation dynamic, the victim begins to identify him/herself in terms of the job or position. The victim's **sources of approval, currency of approval and currency of gratification** all change. The job and its hierarchy become the new, and eventually, the only, source of approval. The currencies of approval that might have once made this person feel proud and fulfilled are replaced by those associated with the job. The currency of gratification begins, more and more, to shift to those things that the job has to offer, usually power, money and prestige.

In other words, the person begins to define him/herself, to find affirmation, in terms of the job, rather than in terms of family, friends, community or group. The person "becomes," in a very real sense, what he or she does. Loyalties shift from the old sources to the new one. It is no longer the job that is interfering with the rest of the person's life, but rather the rest of the person's life that is interfering with the job. It is the job now, and not the spouse, children, community activities or memberships that make the person feel fulfilled. Sometimes, it appears that the person has become money hungry and materialistic. This is an easy assumption to make because that is what most outsiders see. They see the rewards, the money, the new acquisitions, and think that the person's new "devotion" to his/her job can be explained in terms of a hunger for these things. But this is too simplistic an analysis, because there is much more going on here than simply greed. While I do not believe that the "goodies" associated with the position are without effect—remember, they are part of the seductive allure—the question must be asked whether the overachiever is actually enjoying these things. What good is the $700,000 house to someone who is never there? What good is the country club membership to someone who never has time to go there? What good are all the latest electronic toys to someone who never has time to watch a movie or listen to music . . . and would not know what movies are out in any event, because he or she is so totally absorbed in work? So, "greed" and "materialism" are not, in themselves, the complete answer.

It may be, however, that the collection, the acquisition of these things, whether actual physical objects or just an increasing bank account, is the gratifying or fulfilling action. Seeing these objects, reading the bank statement, can be affirming; they can give the person a sense of accomplishment and worth he or she can no longer find elsewhere. Nothing else, not family, home, friends or community involvements fill this need. And so, the job, and its rewards become the affirmation.

For some, it is not the financial rewards of the job that are the affirming factor, but the power and influence the job yields. "Power," Henry Kissinger has been quoted as saying, "is an aphrodisiac." This may be true; but it is also a potent intoxicant for the person who wields it. The vapors of success can turn a person's head just as easily as money can. To have people listen to your every command, fawn over you, always agree with you . . these can be seductive. They can be affirming. They can lead a person to begin to identify him/herself completely with the role he or she plays in an organization.

And so we see how the **affirmation dynamic** can help create one type of seduced **overachiever**.

The second dynamic that leads to this seduction can be a **fear of failure** or the sense of something to prove. Remember, we are not speaking here of the Hollywood/paperback version of the overachiever who was counting his/her first million by age 25. Rather, we're speaking of the successful person who suddenly stepped into a whole new world and got swallowed up by it. For many of these people, studies have shown, there is an underlying fear that he is actually a fraud, that she really isn't up to the demands of the position or the trust placed in her. That he will fail; that she will be exposed. This fear can spur many people into over-achievement because they are continually trying to satis-fy the inner demon of self-doubt.

Similarly, the person might have been a failure in a previous endeavor. He might have come from a poor family or be a member of an ethnic, racial or religious minority. For these reasons and a thousand others, the person may feel that he has something to prove; and overachievement becomes a way to try to do that.

But, of course, since it is the person herself who is applying the pressure, the "proof" will never be sufficient. For no matter how much a person being chased by the inner demon of self-doubt may accomplish, no matter how much he may accomplish or how far he may advance, there will always be more to prove or one more task at which he is afraid he might fail. The seduction in this case is the belief that by overachieving beyond all normal expectations, the failure can be put off; that over-achieving beyond all normal expectations can produce the "proof" of worthiness. Unfortunately, since the fear is self-induced in the first place, no outside influence can satisfy it. The seduction is the process, however, by which the person comes to believe that it can.

The **third** type of seduced overachiever is the one who finds him/herself riding a tiger he/she "dares not dismount."[4] This is the person who has become so seduced by the overachieving lifestyle that he/she cannot imagine living any other way. No matter that he/she is hardly ever in the big house or fancy apartment he/she owns. This person cannot imagine living more simply, without the trappings of success. How strong can this seduction be? When the ex-wife of a certain sports figure committed suicide this past year, her closest friends attributed her action to her inability to live outside of the spotlight, fame and wealth she had shared with her ex-husband.

The sense of being almost trapped by success and its demands is often voiced as "I'm on a treadmill and I don't know how to get off." But this is a dodge, a ruse. The truth is that the person actually fears the gap, getting off that "treadmill" will entail. The person may, for example, not be able to imagine what he/she would do with him/herself if the hours consumed by work were suddenly unoccupied. This fear is not unknown to retirees and those who have been abruptly separated from jobs to which they have devoted their lives. How much stronger must it be for the overachiever who literally fills his/her life with work? This too is a seduction, the job, in this case, having seduced the victim into believing, "You can't live without me."

But not all overachievers are either born to it or are seduced. There is a third type who deliberately uses the demands of overachievement as a **refuge** from other demands, responsibilities or expectations he or she cannot meet. What is the most basic complaint about the overachiever from those living around or with him or her? More often than not, it is that she is completely absorbed in work; that he is emotionally inaccessible and unavailable for commitment because all his energies are focused on his career. But in many cases, this is intentional.

The man who, married and with children, but who wishes he weren't may "overachieve" in order to be unavailable for the demands of marriage and parenthood. The woman, who is too wrapped up in her career to have time for relationships, may be avoiding them because of some deeper fears or issues. The person who, unhappy with himself, pours everything into work, 24/7, may be using the job as an avoidance mechanism to escape who he really is.

In all of these cases, the outside, front-line symptom the world sees is the overachiever devoting the totality of his or her life to the career or the job. This is the person we spoke of earlier in this book; it is the shell we want the world to see. But the **self** behind that mask may be using overachievement and the demands it entails to dodge other issues of responsibility, intimacy and commitment.

So what does this say to the person living or involved with an overachiever? What does this say to the overachiever him/herself?

For those living or involved with the overachiever, unfortunately, these insights are not a magic bullet that will change his or her behavior overnight. But it is important to recognize that yelling, threatening, and acting-out in a negative manner, or even leaving will **NOT** have the impact you hope for. Rather, they will either stiffen the overachiever's resolve not to be sidetracked by your antics, or may, if you leave, actually prove to be both a relief and confirmation that you were only standing in the way of his/her success. You will not gain any ground attacking the **symptom** of overachieving by attacking it head-on, because a symptom is all it usually is. It is the outward manifestation of a larger issue. Often, that issue is the seduction we have been discussing here. Just as often, it is a mask for a fear of failure or a sense of something to prove. If you want to salvage the relationship with the overachiever, these are the issues that must be addressed. The insights offered here will, I hope, help you do that.

And for the overachiever him/herself, what might we say? Coming immediately to mind is the old saying about how few people lying on their deathbed have been quoted as saying, "I just wish I'd spent more time at the office." There is a truth in that statement, but perhaps the words offered to a friend will be more telling.

Upon suddenly finding himself removed from a position with which he had completely identified himself for four years to the total abandonment of the rest of his life, this gentleman was devastated. His identity, he felt, had been stripped from him. Deeply depressed about this, he made a reference to "**his**" office and "**his**" desk, where someone else was now sitting. "That's your mistake," I commented. "It wasn't **your** office. You merely occupied it for a time, as did someone else before you and someone else before him. Only the walls serve forever." Something to think about. . . . .

SOME CLOSING THOUGHTS:

The Long and Winding Road. . . .

≈ ≈ ≈

OK; so here we are, at the end.

And where does that put us?

Hopefully, it has put us in a **better position** than we were in before the journey through this book began. If you remember, when I began this book I talked about the old *Dick Van Dyke Show* and ottomans he used to stumble over during the opening credits each week. I said that we all had psychological and emotional ottomans that we all repeatedly stumbled over, just as poor Dick did. I said I would try to help you move the ones that were blocking your path to personal and professional fulfillment.

Now some of you may be wondering why I didn't just say, "personal and professional *happiness*." The reason is simple: **I can't** make you happy. **I can't do it** and **I'd never promise**. Similarly, you'll notice that I said that I'd "**try to help you**" move the self-generated psychological and emotional obstacles that are in your way; I never said that I would move them. That is something else I can't do and that I'd never promise. Only you can do that; the answer is in you.

And that is what this whole book has been about.

It has been about *your* psychological and emotional obstacles. My job has been to help you identify them, and give you suggestions for avoiding them. But ultimately, how you deal with them is up to **you**.

"*That's it?*" you may ask. "*No answers, no solutions?*"

My reply to that question is, "**No** . . . I would not presume to give you answers and would certainly never presume to try to sell you on the notion that I had **THE** answer to your problems." For the fact is, the <u>truth</u> is, that only you can formulate those answers.

In the introduction to this book, if you recall, I wrote about how a certain friend of mine was complaining that his therapist was "**making him nuts.**" This professional he was seeing, he said, kept suggesting books for him to read, and paradigms for him to follow. Here, he was led to believe, were the answers to his personal and emotional frustrations: this book would solve his romantic and relationship frustrations, that one would solve his problematic relationship with his parents. A book over in the corner would release his spiritual inner being and that one over there would open to the door to self-actualization. Unfortunately, the only one who usually gets actualized from these volumes is the author . . . on his way to the bank to deposit his profits.

By this time, you've probably noticed that I have never once mentioned your inner being, your inner child or your as-yet-unactualized self. Frankly, I think that the vast majority of that stuff is **garbage**. When I set out to write this book I made a promise, to myself and to my readers, that I'd avoid **psychobabble**. I was not going to try to pass off **jargon** as a **substitute for insight**. Did I coin a few new terms? Certainly; the glossary of this book is full of them and they were necessary to describe some important concepts I wanted to discuss. But if you look at each of them, you will find that they are concrete terms for the *real stuff* we all face in *real life*. They are just names I have given to things and processes we're all going through anyhow. **And I think that is what makes this book different**.

I began this book with two basic concepts. The first was that **thought precedes action;** the second was that we usually find ourselves in a **reoccurring chain of negative situations because of the negative, self-defeating behaviors we continually repeat**. Put another way, I believe it is *we*, each of us, that usually set ourselves up for a fall. The negative situations we generally encounter are, more often than not, the products of what we **think** and what we **do**. There are really only three exceptions to this rule. They are negative situations we encounter as the result of:

- an unforeseeable, terrible accident,
- a particularly cruel twist of fate; or
- something someone else does, for whatever reason, to particularly hurt us.

But lets face it: how often, in the scheme of things, are we the victims of such an accident, an outstandingly cruel twist of fate or someone else's intentional, particularly evil action? I'd argue that the answer is, **Not Very Often**. Rather, the disenchantments most of us routinely encounter, those things that generally upset our applecart, ruin our day and can eventually become burdensome, are the products of unmet expectations, disappointments and frustrations. I would further argue that even most of our on-going frustrations with certain situations have more to do with what we think we are not getting out of the situation than they have to do with something that is particularly terrible or onerous about that situation or relationship. To put it another way, the problem is usually not the world; it is usually us. Therefore, the answer is not in a "**paradigm shift**" (whatever the hell *that* is!). It is certainly not in other people. To quote Shakespeare, "the fault . . . is not in our stars, but in ourselves. . . ." Let me give you two examples.

A couple came to see me about the crumbling state of their relationship. Unfortunately, by the time they came to see me, their marriage was really in trouble. He had moved out of their bedroom; they barely spoke to one another. He was suddenly disappearing in the evening and she thought he was having an affair. The problem, it appeared, was his rather sudden dissatisfaction with almost every aspect of his life. He was antagonistic towards her, suddenly detested his job, and was in danger of ruining a perfectly good 15-year career. Yet, when asked what was wrong, he had a host of complaints all focused on her. In time we came to realize that the *real* issue had nothing to do with her, and instead almost completely centered upon his jealousy about one aspect of her job.

Like many other women do when their children are young, this woman had put in almost ten years working at a Major Corporation in a position that was below both her capabilities and aspirations. The trade-off, of course, was that the position did not make extraordinary demands upon her and largely left her free to attend to the children's needs. But when their second child reached fourth grade, this woman, <u>with</u> her husband's backing, resumed the career path upon which she'd been before her children were born. Suddenly, there were not only occasional business dinners she had to attend, but business trips as well; and this was where the problem really started. For while her husband had <u>always</u> traveled for work, his position within state government mandated that his travel was almost exclusively by automobile and within the state. Those few out-of-state trips he took generally saw him driving to a neighboring state capital or occasionally going to New York City by train. By contrast, his wife was suddenly jetting off to Chicago, San Francisco, New Orleans, Atlanta, Colorado, Hawaii, Montreal, Seattle, Vancouver and London. Moreover, where his strict state spending restrictions (and the locales to which he was traveling) severely restricted the accommodations he could enjoy when away on business, she was suddenly enjoying first class hotels in some of the nicest places in the hemisphere.

Ultimately, it turned out that 90% of this couple's problems stemmed from the husband's jealousy over the venues to which his wife was now traveling. Thus, each time she went away on business, he was nastier to her and more disgruntled upon her return. His truly awful behavior was, in essence, an attempt to **"get back"** at her for having taken a trip he wished he could have taken. At work, he was threatening his career by acting out the frustration that his next trip was to be to Elmira and not to San Diego.

In the end, I presented him with four options, really the only options he had.

1. He could divorce her and try to find a woman who would never travel anyplace nicer than he did;
2. He could try to force his wife to quit her new job, which attempt would probably end in said divorce;
3. He could try to find a job similar to the one his wife had, but for which he was thoroughly unprepared and unqualified;

    4. Or, he could work on his attitudes, because the
       problem was largely with him and his percep-
       tion of things.

"The problem," I told him, is not in what she's doing. It is how <u>you</u> are viewing it." In other words, the problem was not one that required the world to change. The problem was not one that required even his wife to change. Rather, the changes needed could only come about within this man himself. But this is not something many of us easily do.

One of the reasons why this is often more difficult than we might think is because we are often compounding the situation through the repetition of a negative pattern. We have all heard of the example where a woman, the daughter of an abusive, alcoholic father, ends up as an adult going through a series of disastrous relationships with abusive, alcoholic men. One reason why that particular example is so well known is because it is fairly easy to see. But not all such patterns are as apparent or readily identified.

As an example, I point to an acquaintance whose professional life was a string of repeated frustrations. Time and again he would be hired for an important, good-paying, high profile position. And as often as he was hired, he'd be let go again within 18-24 months, after coming to grief with his immediate superior. When looking at the particulars of each situation, this person saw little similarity between them. There were aspects, he thought, which made each unique. Not looking for a pattern, he did not see one. But the pattern <u>was</u> there.

In his case, the pattern, the professional ottoman over which he repeatedly tripped, was in seeking employment within highly structured, often highly formal hierarchies. This fellow, it turned out, not only had a real problem with authority figures, but also had never been a joiner. A lone wolf throughout his life, he was a self-motivator and self-starter. In fact, he had realized his greatest career achievements while acting on assignments alone. It was at the end of such assignments, however, when he tried to fit back into the "**normal**" corporate hierarchy, that he invariably came to grief. The problem was not the various supervisors with whom he had come into conflict. The problem was not the "work world." Rather, the problem was in himself, in his unique working style and value system. The answer had two parts. The first was in recognizing the real nature of the problem and its source. The second was in deciding whether he was any longer going to try to be a round peg forced into a square hole.

In the end, he opted for self-employment.

I will offer you a third example. I had a patient a number of years ago. Although she had what many would consider almost a storybook-perfect life, she came to me with that life in complete disarray. In time, we worked through the situation and all seemed well. Two years later, she was back. Once again, her life was falling down around her ears. Again, we worked through the problems and issues and had her on a steady course. Three years later, however, she was back again. Since none of the three circumstances seemed to be connected, we had to look elsewhere if we were to truly address her situation, especially as I do not really believe in "**bad luck**," to which she was ascribing her continuing difficulties.

In time, and after focusing much attention upon her childhood and up bringing, I came to the realization that this woman was **psychologically addicted to high drama**. Tumultuous situations, anguished arguments and heated, tearful confrontations, it turned out, had characterized her parents' relationship and the atmosphere of her childhood. In short, this woman found normalcy to be boring. The more settled a situation became, the more she found it to be stifling. The less crisis there was in her life, the more she found that life to be confining. Having a loving, caring husband and a stable relationship, she longed for the uncertainty and novelty (and thus the excitement) of her dating days. Having arrived at a point in her career where she was secure, she missed the challenge of having to prove herself. Having attained a position of respect in her community, she missed her teenage image of disreputable town rebel. The pattern was within her; the "**problem**" was within her. The answer, in the end, was **within her**.

If we think about it, I believe that many, if not most, of the real life issues we stumble over each day are like the ones we have been discussing throughout this book; they come from within ourselves. They come from something we are doing, something we are not doing, or from something we are vainly expecting to happen. So if this is where the majority of our frustrations have their origin, doesn't it make sense to start there in our search for solutions?

Now, none of this is to say that change is easy. People usually want others to change first. They want the situation to change to their liking. But this rarely happens, and even when it does, it usually does not solve the deeper problem or address the base issues. Our friend who resented the world-class hotels in which his wife was staying might be temporarily satisfied if she started staying at Motel-6, but that would not resolve the deeper issues. In the end, unless **he** changed the way he was viewing things, he'd be resentful no matter how many changes she made. Moreover, recognizing the changes we need to make, and even making them, does not mean that we will *ever* actually like the thing or the situation, which now makes us angry or resentful. The fellow we are discussing will probably <u>never</u> "like" the fact that his wife is jetting off to Maui or Miami on business while he's driving a stripped-down sub-compact from the state auto pool to Utica in a snowstorm. But if he recognizes the fact that the real source of his negative feelings is that he is jealous, and not that she is ignoring him, abandoning her responsibilities or having an affair, he has a better chance of addressing those feelings rather than having them control him and lead to the ruination of an essentially sound and loving marriage.

🐌 🐌 🐌

Over the course of this book's nineteen chapters, I have tried to illustrate how the things we think and do impact our lives. I have tried to offer warning signs. I have tried to offer approaches to common problems that bedevil most of us. I have not offered ironclad, sure-fire, guaranteed answers. I have not offered completely certain solutions. Guarantees shrink with the small print; few things in this life are really ironclad or sure-fire. And as Ben Franklin observed, in this world only death and taxes are completely certain.

So where does that leave us?

It leaves me having done the best I can do; I hope it has been helpful.

It leaves you with some **choices** you probably have to make; I hope you make the most of them.

🌱 🌱 🌱

NOTES

[1] Peter, Laurence J. and Raymond Hull.   Morrow, William and Company (May 1976).

[2] There is a very large body of both scholarly and popular literature on this subject. I present here a sample, much of which the reader may conveniently access.

Modern Beauty: Successes and Failures (http://www.gened.arizona.edu/maccorqu/student_work/dan.htm);

Brumberg, Joan Jacobs. *The Body Project: An Intimate History of American Girls*. Random House, New York, New York, 1997;

Lakoff, Robin Tolmach and Raquel L. Scherr, *Face Value: The Politics of Beauty*. Routledge and Kegan, New York, 1984;

Landau, Elaine. *The Beauty Trap*.   MacMillan Publishing Company, New York, New York, 1994;

Sanford, Linda T. and Mary Ellen Donovan. *Women and Self-Esteem*. The Penguin Group, New York, New York, 1984;

Gustafson, Robert and Mark Popovich.   *Eating Disorders Among High School Girls* (http://www.journalism.bsu.edu/Journalism/Alumni/PhoenixSpg00Mark_Bob.html);

Henss, R. *The Big Five and Physical Attractiveness*. Presented at the 8th European Conference on Personality.   Ghent, Belgium, July 8-12, 1996.   (http://www.cops.unisaar-land.de/ronald/PUBLICAT/ABSTRACT/EAPP96.HTM);

Steele. "A threat in the air: How stereotypes shape intellectual identity and performance." *American Psychologist* 52 (1997): 713-729;

Budesheim and DePaula. "Beauty or the beast? The effects of appearance, personality, and issue information on evaluations of political candidates." *Personality and Social Psychology Bulletin* 20 (1994): 339-348;

Shahani, Dipboye and Gehrlein. "Attractiveness bias in the interview: Exploring the boundaries of an effect." *Basic and Applied Social Psychology* 14 (1993): 317-328.

[3] http://fb.women.com/fashionandbeauty/fashion/imgtalk/b9beau11.htm).

[4] Scarborough, William. Chinese Proverbs (1875), no. 2082: "He who rides a tiger is afraid to dismount."

GLOSSARY

≈ ≈ ≈

Authority figure: A person or group of persons we allow to have *effective control* over at least some portion of the actions that comprise our lives.

Cognitive dissonance: The often-upsetting realization that what we firmly believe is not true; that what we think we know is inaccurate, misguided or simply wrong.   Goes beyond knowledge of mere facts to more deeply held beliefs, trusts and expectations.   An incongruity between what we believe (is, should be, or will be) and what we, perhaps belatedly, know to be the case.

Conditioned thinking: A learned, patterned, often subconscious response to stimuli.

Conscious competence: The stage of what we know in an active, "I'm-using-this-knowledge-right-this minute" sort of way.

Conscious incompetence: The awareness of knowledge one does not possess.

Contradiction: A discontinuity between a goal and the conditions under which one is trying to achieve that goal.

Currencies of approval: The differing forms through which we seek, recognize and accept approval throughout our lives.

Currencies of gratification: Those things, differing over time and changing as we grow and mature, that satisfy us and make us happy.

Denial: The active refusal to accept what *is*.

Effective control: The ability to unquestioningly dictate major and significant aspects of a situation or another person's actions.

Ego bruise: A set of circumstances that damages your self-concept.

Facilitating our environment: The process of identifying a goal, identifying the parts over which we have some potential for control and doing everything we reasonably can to improve our chances of realizing that goal by exercising the control we have.

Individuation: The breaking away from the patterns and bonds that largely described childhood.

Merging authority figures: The end condition resulting from a process whereby the place, role, rights and relationship with a person's primary authority figure are extended to all other actual or commonly accepted authority figures in a person's life.

Operating assumption: A set of expectations based on concrete experience and a rational assessment of probable events and outcomes.

Operating attitudes: Those senses of self-competence and ability with which we face the world; a mental and emotional measuring stick assessing risk and the probabilities of success for us each time we face a challenging situation.

Operating fantasies: A set of expectations based more on wish fulfillment than on concrete experience and a rational assessment of probable events and outcomes.

Operating presumptions: A set of expectations that go beyond a rational, realistic assumption of an outcome over which one has some degree of control, to an additional, secondary outcome over which one has no control.

Overachiever: Someone who not only achieves a goal, but does so to a degree and with a consistency that most people do not. An observable behavioral pattern.

Parallel value tracks: Subconscious or emotional tools for managing increasingly segmented lives. Self-contained sets of values and norms of behavior we apply to separate situations and relationships.

Person **and** *Self*:   The differentiation between who we really are and what we feel on the inside (the self) and who the world sees and interacts with (the person).

Projection: The process by which we ascribe to or anticipate from another person feelings and attitudes that actually originate within us.

Recognition: An acknowledgment, most often intangible, of one's actions or performance.

Reward: A tangible benefit derived from one's actions or performance.

Rites of passage: Milestones, defining moments in our lives. These can take the form of an event or can be legally, physically or symbolically ascribed a meaning or value.

Self-concept: A sense of self. How we see ourselves, our sense of self-value and the treatment to which we are entitled.

Shaping pattern: Those events and circumstances, particularly in early childhood, that begin to form our personalities and who we will become in the future.

Social lie: Words or actions specifically designed to hide or mask our true feelings about a situation in favor of a socially acceptable façade of competence, happiness, acquiescence or pleasure.

Sources of approval: Those people, institutions or situations to which we look for validation of our worth, place and self.

Standards of approval: Those things or actions for which we are rewarded.

Stimulus: An activating event, something that stimulates our subconscious brain to answer in some way.

Thought reinforcement: The process by which our subconscious mind manufactures substantiation for a self-generated, often projected feeling.

Unconscious competence: The stage at which we no longer think about what we know.

Unconscious incompetence: Unawareness of an inability to do something.

Well-formed outcome: A targeted, beneficial result of one's actions. By definition, something over which one has at least a potential for some degree of control.

About the Author

Mark Hillman, Ph.D., has been a counselor/coach/mentor in private practice since 1982. He is devoted to helping individuals, families and business corporations resolve crisis and conflict. He started his career as the Director of the Veterans Educational Program in Albany, New York, then spent seven years in public education and since, has been providing private consultations for the past 21 years.

As an individual and corporate therapist, he is a much sought after consultant and speaker, providing a wide range of services for positive change. He has been published nationally, and recently provided training seminars in Russia.

He offers an array of services including:

- Individual, Marriage & Family Counseling
- Peak Performance Training

- Strategic Mentoring
- Systematic Management
- Systems to Success
- Executive Coaching
- Strategic Thinking
- Creativity Training
- Tactical Planning
- Team Building

Originally from New York City, he is married and has two daughters, and presently resides in Clifton Park, New York.

❧ ❧ ❧

For more information on the wide range of resources available from Mark Hillman, Ph.D., visit his website at:

www.drmarkhillman.com

or call, e-mail, write or fax:

Dr. Mark Hillman
531 Moe Road
Clifton Park, New York   12065

Toll Free:	1-877-865-3003
Fax:	518-383-4101
Phone:	518-383-4100
E-mail:	drmark@drmarkhillman.com

To Order Books

Please mail, fax, or e-mail your order:

___ copies at $19.95 each = _____
        ($19.95 U.S. currency; $24.95 in Canada)

Plus $4.50 each shipping/handling = _____
        ($4.50 U.S. currency; $6.00 in Canada)

New York State Residents please add 8% ($1.96)
Sales Tax per book.

Total enclosed = _____

Please send books to:

NAME: _____
ADDRESS: _____
CITY: _____, STATE: _____, ZIP: _____

_____ VISA   _____ MASTERCARD

Credit Card Number _____
Expiration Date _____   Phone # _____
Cardholder's signature _____

Order by sending credit card, check or money order to:

Dr. Mark Hillman
531 Moe Road
Clifton Park, NY   12065
1-877-865-3003
        518-383-4100 (Office)
        518-383-4101 (Fax)
        drmark@drmarkhillman.com (e-mail)
        Visit our website: www.drmarkhillman.com